Glimpses of the Beyond

Glimpses

Delacorte Press/New York

of the Beyond

The Extraordinary Experiences of People Who
Have Crossed the Brink of Death and Returned

Jean-Baptiste Delacour

Translated from the German by E.B. Garside

Contents

A Necessary Word of Introduction

THE DARKLING THRESHOLD between being and what seems to be not-being—the reef on which life goes aground, only to set sail on a new journey into the unknown—since time's beginning has aroused intense curiosity in mankind. The quest for un-equivocal evidence and clear answers has always been with us. Our civilization tries to drive death from the human con-sciousness, yet at some time or other everyone becomes wrapped up in the question.

So far there is no final scientific determination proving that when a person dies everything is absolutely finished. Neither is there any proof, unequivocal and independent of faith, of the existence of a something that lives on after death despite the body's decay. Thus, the seeker is torn between the inadequate findings of science and the myriad interpretations of world religions old and new. He casts about for any ray of light emanating out of darkness, for any evidence that something in us does last beyond death, or that gives some inkling as to what existence after death might be like.

Unsteady planks of bridges leading whither no one sees or knows, floating bits rising up out of murky depths, mirages in which the bright images of hopeful fantasy are closely inter-mingled with the anxiety dreams of sick minds—all these we have brought together into a mosaic. For there have been and are people who have stood on this threshold and who affirm—who personally are completely convinced—that they have been "out yonder" on the other side and made a return from this other state of being.

We shall repeat word for word what they have recounted about their experiences on "the other side." Each of you can then judge for yourself and bring your own point of view to bear—the critical reader, the doubting psychologist, the ice-cold nay-sayer on principle.

Only one thing: None of you should look at this matter too simplistically or reject out of hand everything that can be recounted of another world—a subject that, after all, has engrossed the wisest minds of all ages.

Who can discriminate errorlessly between reality and the flickering tremors of a spirit clinging desperately to this world; between actual experience and a dying person's wishful images; between true events and the hallucinations of someone clinically dead, whose brain was perhaps already subjected to physiological change before chance or medical art restored him to life? It is not impossible to interrogate the brain about life after death, or, at any rate, about what so many designate as such. The brain lives differently and longer than science has heretofore believed.

Even quite some time ago doubts were stirring about the early onset of irreversibility in the death of the brain *intra vitam*, that is, while other parts of the body are still technically alive. Wishful thoughts about making death reversible are as old as man. The experiments of University of Cologne docent Dr. Konstantin Hossmann, who works with Professor Dr. Klaus Zülch, head of the Max Planck Institute of Brain Research at Cologne-Merheim, have shown that signs of life can be restored in brain cells deprived of a blood supply for an hour or more. Later these experiments will be gone into more thoroughly. But suffice it to say for now, these inquiries contradict the previously held opinion that an absence of blood leads to irreversible brain damage after only eight to ten minutes. Previously the only possibility admitted to was that in some cases of sudden death by accident or acute illness, the circulation of the blood and breathing could again be set in motion after long periods by the use of modern resuscitation methods. But the brain cells—we were assured—were irrevocably dead.

An experimental team under Dr. Hossmann carried out inquiries—using complicated experimental techniques (first on
animals)—aimed at finding out just what structural and functional changes did occur in the brain when the blood supply is
cut off for more than ten minutes. It was determined that brain
cells become irreparably damaged much later than had previously been supposed. They still reacted positively once the
blood supply was restored after an hour, and even longer.

Obviously, the absence of blood gives rise to changes in the
brain's blood vessels, that is to say, to a marked contraction. But
with the aid of ingeniously devised experimental techniques,
Dr. Hossmann and his colleagues were able to reduce the contraction effect. This made it possible to restore cerebral
functions.

What was done experimentally at the Max Planck Institute
of Brain Research in Cologne-Merheim can come about naturally under certain conditions and lead to the revival of a person already declared clinically dead.

Thus, what many of those who claim to have been on "the
other side" are saying, at the very least, is not concocted
testimony invented after the fact, but an actual cerebral experience, something registered by the "I," the self, when it
went on a strange journey during a period of clinical death.

With those who have tried to put this experience into words,
we shall wander over this narrow threshold where dark depths
and luminous heights, this world and the beyond, far and near,
become one and have no boundaries, no time, no end.

The seeker who reads these accounts perhaps will find a
tentative foothold here and there. He will, at any rate, come to
know, for what he may think it worth, what those people say
who have been chosen by fate to stumble across the narrow
threshold and then come back from the dead to tarry in this
world.

In a cemetery in a small south German town, there is a
gravestone on which a simple man, remembered now only by
his name and the dates of his birth and death, had had his last
testament chiseled in the stone:

"Now I know more than the wisest among you."

But is it not possible that the depositions of the clinically dead who lived again may modify this sentiment?

The Munich philosopher Arnold Metzger in his monograph *Freedom and Death* writes:

"Man has a knowledge of his own existence, and in this knowledge transcends the moment when he goes out beyond the world. The free being breaks the power of death."

The mathematician-philosopher Pythagoras once said: "The soul of man is divided into three parts: intelligence, reason, and passion. Animals also have intelligence and passion, but only man has reason. Reason is imperishable, all else is mortal."

Shall we try, with our immortal reason, to lift the veil that shrouds the "other world"?

He who does not want to die should not want to live. For life is tendered to us with the proviso of death; life is the way to this destination. On this account, it is folly to fear death; for only the uncertain is to be feared, the certain being taken for granted. Death signifies a just and unavoidable necessity. Who should complain about a situation in which everyone is unexceptionable? The first law of justice is equality. Therefore, it would be unseemly to reproach Nature for not having a different law for us than for herself. What she joins together, she puts asunder, and what she puts asunder she joins together again.

LUCIUS ANNAEUS SENECA (c. 3 B.C.–A.D. 65)

1

"I'm Not Afraid
of Dying Any More!"

THE MAN LAY in the easy chair with his shirt collar torn open
and both hands clawing at his chest. He had not put the phone
back on the hook. He was thrashing about on the floor when the
waiter burst into the room.

The man opened his mouth, but only a faint groan crossed
his lips. Naked fear stood in his eyes.

The next moment his head, the face ghastly pale, fell to one
side, his cramped fingers relaxed, and his arms fell limp.

A doctor was called, an ambulance hurriedly summoned.
The unconscious victim was taken, blue ambulance lights
flashing, to the Danolo Hospital in Tel Aviv.

The man who, with his last ounce of strength, reached for
the phone in his luxury hotel suite that twenty-ninth of June,
1971, and in an almost unintelligible whisper called for help
was the French actor Daniel Gélin, in earlier years a movie
star known throughout Europe.

As so often in years past, he had come to Israel for the inter-
national film festival. Never before had he been bothered by
the dry heat, which during the summer months sometimes
makes Tel Aviv unbearable for a northern European.

But in May he had marked his fiftieth birthday. Fifty years
old—a dangerous time of life, especially for a man looking back
on a career whose heights and depths had taken a toll.

Let Gélin himself describe his ensuing experiences in the
Danolo Hospital:

"I came to with agonizing pains in the region of the heart.

A figure dressed in white, who I now know was a doctor, was standing in front of me. Then a black curtain abruptly dropped before my eyes. I was dead, without being immediately clear about it. Only one thing struck me: Although not yet free of pain, I could feel that the load which for hours had been threatening to burst my chest had been taken from me. Was getting up all I needed to do to resume my normal life?

"While I was looking around, something strange happened to me.

"Suddenly I found myself floating through the room. I moved like a shadow over to the apparatus recording my heartbeat, and was horrified to see that the needle wasn't moving. My heart had come to a dead stop.

"I opened my mouth to ask a question about this, but no sound came from my lips.

"The doctor was leaning over the bed. From my floating state I became aware that down there was my body, lying supine. The doctor was giving it an intravenous injection. He waited to see if it would have any effect. When nothing happened, he sighed and turned away. His female assistant pulled up the sheet and covered my face.

"At this moment in terror I began to plead: 'Save me! Don't leave me for dead!'

"But it was impossible to make myself understood. No one was hearing what I was screaming with all my strength. After I saw how futile my efforts were, I tried another way. In thought I clung to everything I held dear. With all the concentration my mind was capable of, I fastened my thoughts on my children. But this stratagem proved futile too, for the faces I tried to visualize came to me only fleetingly, nebulously. I murmured my children's names like a litany: Zazie, Manuel, Fiona—always in the same sequence: Zazie, Manuel, Fiona.

"Nothing happened. No one came to my aid, and I had to face up to the fact that everything that had been my life and happiness on earth stayed far from me.

"I had reached a point of great despair and aloneness since becoming separated from my body. When I was alive, death had held no terrors for me. But the emptiness in which I now found myself trapped was horrible.

"In my new, post-mortem state I had become light and insubstantial. Everything in my surroundings was new to me. The minute I moved I stirred up a cloud of fine, gleaming dust. The little particles made me think of stardust. The sky now arching over me like a dome was preternaturally clear and a very light blue color that seemed pure and transparent.

"Gradually a certain cheerfulness replaced my initial despair. I'm a Breton and a believer, in the Christian sense.

"The shadows or shades who suddenly were all around me gave me the notion they must have something to do with my parents, and presently I actually recognized my father and mother among them. A boundless joy filled my heart. Death had taken my parents from me, one after the other in a brief span. They had been buried side by side in St.-Malo, where they had spent their lives—St.-Malo, the town of my childhood and youth.

"It was an unimaginable miracle for me to find my parents again under the great sun of a happy hereafter.

"Only gradually did the outlines of my father and mother become more distinct and finally take on firm shape before my astonished eyes. My father, with the deep, weatherworn furrows in his face, and my mother, reserved and dainty with a tender smile, as I had known her in those days; there they were, right in front of me. A deep feeling of happiness came over me as I saw I could take them both in my arms.

"But it seemed to me that I could look forward to an even greater joy. For now my mother made the same kind of gesture I had known her to make when I was a child, when she would take me by the hand to go for a walk down to the harbor, where the river Rance flows by little islands and rocks into the sea, or through the narrow streets and alleys of our little city, which is built on a jutting cliff. This time she led me to a mysterious place that I certainly would never have discovered by myself, without her providential help.

"We found ourselves in a rose-colored world, a sort of fairy garden filled with wonderful flowers. Children were playing and laughing on every side. Suddenly I heard my mother whisper: 'Pascal is here. See how happy he feels.'

"Now I saw him too: Pascal, my son, taken from us at the age of fourteen months by a tragic accident. His face was round and rosy, his hair fair, hands small and plump. My child's death, when it happened, almost killed me. Now I found him again, as a smiling little boy in the magical frame of this otherworldly garden. He stumbled toward me in a rush, his little legs still not used to walking.

"Tears of joy streamed from my eyes and a deep, warm feeling of happiness flowed through me. Nonetheless, I had to think back to that terrible day in the hospital corridor when a nun told me there had been no possibility of saving him. The dose of sleeping tablets he'd swallowed in an unwatched moment had been fatal.

"At the time the sister had said, by way of consolation: 'Now he is an angel in heaven.'

"These words had had a shock effect on me. In my anguish I had automatically raised my hand to give the sister a box on the ear.

"Now I realized the nun had been right and that death did not represent a hideous end to life. I had discovered there was more than a melancholy, bereft nothingness to existence after death.

"In my rapture I started to run toward Pascal to fold him in my arms. But when my hand touched him, everything around me changed. Both little Pascal and my father disappeared. The only one remaining clearly recognizable was my mother. When I realized that everything I had just been perceiving had ended up by vanishing like a mirage, I began loudly to cry out in despair. Then I heard my mother saying to me, with an undertone of sadness: 'Go now, Daniel, it's time, life is waiting.'

"But what did I want with life now? Just as earlier in the clinic I had fought against death with all my might, now I put up a fierce battle against returning to the living. I wanted to stay where I was.

"I ranted and raved like a madman for Pascal, whom I'd now lost a second time. All in vain. An inexorable force bore me away. My screams and shouts were lost in a boundless world without light and color. I could again feel agonizing pain. I became excruciatingly preoccupied with my heart.

"I let out a final scream, opened my eyes, and knew I was still alive.

"My head was filled with a yawning emptiness, and I felt extraordinarily weak. I was now able to identify the doctor at my bedside as the white figure that earlier I had seen bending over my body. When had that been, really? Minutes ago, hours, days?

"When I started to inquire, the nurse put a finger on her lips, signaling me to keep still. She and the doctor had a look of relief on their faces.

"So I closed my eyes again, in secret expectation of seeing my mother's smile again, my father's stern face, and little Pascal, happy as could be. But instead I must have fallen into a deep, dreamless sleep.

"When I woke up in an oxygen tent, I tried to get the doctor to explain what he had done, what measures he had taken to snatch me from death.

"I took it for granted that I wouldn't tell him about my experiences in the other world—not at this time, when he had just done everything to save my life. In the same spirit, several weeks later, I gave up the idea of talking about it to my nurse. I merely asked her if they'd really thought I was dead and covered my face with a sheet. I can still see the nurse—her smile, the impenetrable look on her face. All she would say was they were much too busy at that hospital to bother about dead people. Certainly, she was not one who would ever take much stock in any account of mine of life after death. Therefore, I said nothing."

Immediately, in connection with this incident, one remembers the film *The Man Who Knew Too Much*, in which Daniel Gélin played one of the many roles that made him famous.

Gélin made his big breakthrough in 1948 with *Rendezvous*

Latin Quarter and soon afterward was chosen by the philosopher-dramatist of world note, Jean-Paul Sartre, for the leading role in his film *Dirty Hands*, which the self-willed existentialist personally directed.

Daniel Gélin played contemporary characters with a felicitous naturalness—now the jealous husband or love-smitten student, now the frustrated idealist or the dying secret agent disguised as an Arab; the attic bohemian of Montmartre, or the enigmatic holdup man who, in his daring, breaks into the house of the only witness against him, to flirt with the man's wife and finally to maneuver the man before the Arab magistrate, to make the accuser himself the defendant.

Gélin's big black eyes looked out everywhere from moviehouse placards and magazine covers—eyes that could be as wise and searching as at other times cunning, sly, or skeptical.

The set of his nose and his small mouth reflected all the willfulness of his Breton character, a character meeting all difficulties and obstacles with an iron-hard "I will."

In his private life, womanizing was not his thing. He was completely engrossed in his career. However, one day he met a woman with whom he fell head over heels in love and whom—as is common among actors—he married on the spot.

Once, Daniel Gélin cautiously indicated the disappointments the years of marriage to Danielle Delorme had brought him.

"She played her parts not only on stage, but at home as well."

Meanwhile, the film fans, all those countless women and girls who had made an idol of this glittering star in the cinematic heavens, saw only one side of Gélin: He had everything that made life worthwhile—talent, fame, wealth, and a most attractive woman, a woman millions of men envied him for.

And then, abruptly, Daniel Gélin moved into the shadows.

Hardly anyone deliberately chooses to become an alcoholic or drug user. Almost always it is raw life itself that drives people to the bottle or the needle.

At the beginning, all that he wanted was to cope with a personal crisis and artistic depression, a state of exhaustion. But the feelings of bliss he found made him, at the height of his triumphs, a victim of whiskey and heroin.

The reason for his sudden decline quickly leaked out from the studios, where he was seen ever less frequently before the cameras. The comedian with the many-sided potential for masterly projections, the face so full of mystery, was quickly forgotten.

Until, one day, into his trembling hands came a scenario for a new film. This time he was to play himself: a drug addict. He was to act out his whole life, his past and the stretch of road still lying before him—play it all to the bitter end.

He was at first filled with loathing for the script. But then it suddenly occurred to him that it could be his salvation.

At the same time he thought of a woman, Sylvia. "Reach out to her, take the hand she's offering you—before it's irretrievably too late."

For Sylvia, that brave creature, wanted to help him. All the others despised him, humiliated him. Everyone had given up on him: friends, fellow actors, producers, and even his own wife, Danielle.

Before, he had retreated from Sylvia and scorned her help—until this manuscript offered him a last chance.

In moving words Daniel Gélin has described his way back into society at Sylvia's side. She and his children together helped him conquer the dread fear of a relapse.

Anyone who knows Gélin's life story will understand the relationships that are thematic in his account of his fascinating journey into the beyond. This report closes with these words:

"If at times I feel weak or depressed, I think back on the kingdom of the dead. I shut my eyes, and the luminous life that was revealed to me comes back as an unforgettable reality . . ."

What Daniel Gélin had to relate differs only in detail from other impressive accounts left by all those who found death pleasant and who did not wish to come back to earthly existence.

A case in point is the seventy-six-year-old widow who

strengthened New York Dr. Frank Cosmos's belief in the promise of a finer world in the beyond.

Betty Patterson died as the result of a burst appendix, but was revived a few minutes later on the operating table. Her first words were: "I'll never be afraid of dying again." To which she added:

"At first I felt as if my spirit, my self, was separating from the husk of my body and floating up to the ceiling of the room. From up there I could look down at my body on the operating table. Then this scene vanished from my field of view, and suddenly I was surrounded by gentle light and soft music. I was overcome by a feeling of deep content that I had never felt in life. This sensation overpowered me in such a way that I no longer felt any desire for earthly life. I tried to move in the direction the sounds were coming from, but something forcibly prevented me. Apparently, the time had not come for the final separation from my body."

James Lorne, forty-seven, had a similar experience in Los Angeles.

After suffering a heart attack, he was dead for a period of five minutes. The physician in charge, Dr. Samuel Kassmann, did not question the authenticity of the statements about to follow. He had known Lorne for years as an honest patient whose sober nature did not admit of superstitious notions or mystical happenings.

"I felt myself floating in the air and could clearly see my body lying down there. I landed in a long corridor filled with soft twilight. At the end a bright light was shining. I could also hear voices coming from there.

"When I reached the end of the tunnel or corridor, I came out into a splendid garden with trees bearing all kinds of fruit. Stretching out, too, before my eyes were meadows with bright flowers in bloom. Everywhere people were standing about in groups, conversing together. But when I began to move closer, the scene always receded in front of me. Nobody seemed to be aware of my shouts, my desire to stay there."

Later, when James Lorne saw his wife and children standing

at his bedside with sad and apprehensive mien, he felt he knew why fate had sent him back into life. Yet he assured them:

"When one day the time comes for me really to die, I won't try to resist. I'll be ready to follow the call into the beyond."

Do not worry about what the future may bring, but strive to become firm and clear within. For it is not how fate fashions it, but how you come to terms with fate that will bring your life's happiness.

Georg Wilhelm Friedrich Hegel (1770–1831)

2

A Ballerina Sees into the Future

THE CAMERAS HUMMED, and the spotlights in the television studio followed the beautiful ballerina as, white and slender, she swirled about the stage like a great snowflake.

Suddenly things began to happen so fast that nobody knew what was happening or why: a terrible cracking sound; a red glow in the glaring light; scenery in flames; and a wraith of tulle and spangles, a living torch.

The unconscious woman was rushed to the nearest Paris emergency clinic with third-degree burns.

The doctors could find no pulse. Blood was no longer circulating. The last throb of life seemed to have left the hideously damaged body. But these specialists, always ready to deal with acute emergencies, did everything they considered to be a last obligation, even for someone clinically dead. She was given oxygen, circulatory aids, and above all, massage to set the stopped heart in motion.

By now the heart had been stopped for more than a minute, but they continued to work on both it and the blackened burns. From time to time there seemed to be a glimmer of hope, though in truth they would have been justified in giving up.

Thus Janine Charrat, as if by a miracle, was brought back to life.

But what did the dancer experience during those minutes on December 18, 1961, when her body was completely lifeless?

After these many years, she can still remember every detail.

"I was overcome by a dizzy, whirling feeling, and I thought I was falling into a deep well. The fall seemed never to end, and all my attempts to catch hold of something were in vain. When I finally felt ground under my feet, I could open my eyes again, which before had been shut fast by lids as heavy as lead.

"But what was now revealed to me made me cry out loudly in terror. I was alone in a strange and unfamiliar world, surrounded by huge licking flames. The flames got bigger, and their incandescent redness became so glaring that I thought I would perish of fear.

"It really and truly had to be hell!

"The thick curtain of fire had to be the devil's work, for how else were the leaping flames being fed? They seemed to be coming in a wild dance out of the interior of the earth, their bizarre shapes constantly changing. The ground under me was incandescent, a lavalike, boiling mud.

"In the face of my great aloneness and the growing danger of the flames, I was suddenly gripped by a powerful determination to put an end to this menacing situation. I steeled myself to walk right up to the flames. Doing this I noticed that the glowing surface underfoot was only moderately warm. I came to a standstill immediately at the wall of flame encircling me, meanwhile remembering the fiery catastrophe I had just been through on the stage. As a believer, I have always prayed in dangerous situations, and that is what I turned to now.

"After saying prayers, I lifted my head and noted that the tall flames were no longer terrifying. They had become much smaller and only a rosy color, and almost transparent. Now all fear left me. I strode through the circle of fire and at once felt a great relief. Although I was aware of still having awful burns, I felt no more pain.

"While I was taking these first steps into the mysterious world behind the fire curtain, I suddenly found myself looking about in despair for another human presence. How would I ever manage alone and helpless in these strange surroundings? Scarcely had this yearning for company come into my mind when I caught sight of a woman in a silk dress. Her white hair was done up, her brown eyes were mild, and a kind, concerned smile played about her lips.

"With slow movements this woman floated toward me and began to speak, saying:

"'You don't remember me, then, Janine? I'm Isabelle, your grandmother. Have you forgotten me?'

"Now I did recognize my dead grandmother, and felt wonderfully happy to have her with me in my sorry state.

"She took me tenderly by the arm and gave me the following explanation, in my ignorance of the subject, of how things were in this afterworld and what the rules were here: 'In the land of the dead everything is written down—the past, the present, and the future, too . . . Each person's fate is recorded in the heavenly book of life. At this moment you may feel lost. Because of that, I'm going to show you something that, I hope, will restore your courage—for you're going to need all the courage and trust you can muster.'

"Without hesitation I followed as she led the way. We walked along through a reddish mist and came into a big garden where there were many fantastic trees unknown to me, a place filled with a marvelous harmony. In the middle of the garden was a pond. The water in the pond was calm and clear and remarkably clean. The pond was like a mirror filled with light.

"My grandmother urged me to bend down over the pond's surface. When I looked down into it more closely, I observed images taking shape on the watery surface. I soon realized I was seeing two nurses who were going to hold me up when I made my first attempts to walk again. Explaining this to me, my grandmother said: 'It will be a long time before you are well again. Keep on looking into the pool. You must use every opportunity you have here.'

"These words seemed so important to me that I kept my eyes glued to the pure liquid surface. I saw visions of coming years, visions that unrolled before me like a film. I saw myself getting married on an island in the South Seas. For the marriage ceremony I was wearing a crown of flowers, according to native custom. The bridegroom standing beside me was a total stranger, a man considerably taller than myself. I heard myself call him Michel, and was conscious that this other self

of mine was radiant with happiness. All this seemed hardly
credible, since I knew perfectly well I was still married to the
screen actor Gérard Munsky. Though, to be sure, for some
time we had been having many differences, and were no
longer on good terms. As a matter of fact, we had already
agreed on a divorce. Yet I couldn't believe I would enter into
another marriage.

"Watching these images reflected in the water, doubt crept
in, and I wondered whether I was really seeing my future. I
would have to ask my grandmother. But when I looked up to
her, she was no longer to be seen. My euphoria vanished; my
limbs felt dead tired and heavy as lead. In this state of exhaustion, my burns began to turn fiery again, and I hurt so
much that I groaned with pain.

"I must now have suddenly returned to consciousness. I
opened my eyes, and there I was, lying on a white hospital
bed."

A long period of suffering began for Janine Charrat. The
chances of saving a patient with such extensive burns were
slight. The enormous loss of albumin and plasma in the burned
areas and the poisons produced in the albumin by the burns
and disturbances in the skin's heat control system lead to intense shock, which can rapidly lead to circulatory and cardiac
failure. But as it turned out, in this case the doctors were
finally able to boast of a success they could have hardly
dreamed of at the start.

Janine Charrat, with iron will, overcame the loathsome and
agonizing consequences of the deficient functioning of affected
organs (especially the liver), and bore up well under the painful treatment of the wounds and the various skin transplants.

Only a few of the patrons of night clubs and variety shows
know the story of the celebrated dancer, an artist who has
never needed to worry about engagements. When she first re-
appeared on the stage after her recovery, nobody noticed the
marks left by the accident. And shortly after this return to
dancing, in Geneva she met a tall man who thereafter wished
never to leave her side. Janine Charrat and Michel Humbert

were married in August, 1969, in Haapiti, a small village on the South Pacific island of Mooréa.

The years following the burning accident in the Paris TV studio unfolded just as they had been prefigured in the mirror of the future in the afterworld, and Janine Charrat claims to this day that only this experience gave her the fortitude and patience to hold out during the year-long recuperation process.

Similar to the experiences reported by the French prima ballerina Charrat are descriptions of a mysterious contact with the afterworld by the German actor Curt Jurgens.

Curt Jurgens had come to Houston, Texas, to consult with one of President Eisenhower's personal cardiologists about a severe heart ailment.

Dr. Michael E. De Bakey advised Jurgens to submit to a replacement of the aorta with a plastic artery about 7.9 inches long. He accompanied this advice with a grave warning about the surgical risk.

Although the chance of survival was rated at only 50 percent, the patient, who is known as a man hard on others but even harder on himself, decided to have the four-hour operation.

With the help of assistants, De Bakey had to take the heart out of circulation and then replace the defective aortic artery with a plastic tube. Finally, the heart had to be set going again. In effect, Curt Jurgens was dead for several minutes. His impressions of this brief sojourn in the supernatural world he has described in his own words as follows:

"The feeling of well-being that I had shortly after the pentothal injection did not last long. Soon a feeling that life was ebbing from me rose up from the subconscious. Today I like to say that this sensation came at the moment my heart stopped beating. Feeling my life draining away evoked powerful sensations of dread. I wanted to hold on to life more than anything, yet it was impossible for me to do so. I had been looking up into the big glass cupola over the operating room. This cupola now began to change. Suddenly it turned a glowing red. I saw twisted faces grimacing as they stared down at me.

Overcome by dread, I tried to struggle upright and defend myself against these pallid ghosts, who were moving closer to me. Then it seemed as if the glass cupola had turned into a transparent dome that was slowly sinking down over me. A fiery rain was now falling, but though the drops were enormous, none of them touched me. They splattered down around me, and out of them grew menacing tongues of flames licking up about me. I could no longer shut out the frightful truth: Beyond doubt, the faces dominating this fiery world were faces of the damned. I had a feeling of despair, of being unspeakably alone and abandoned. The sensation of horror was so great it choked me, and I had the impression I was about to suffocate.

"Obviously I was in Hell itself, and the glowing tongues of fire could be reaching me any minute. In this situation, the black silhouette of a human figure suddenly materialized and began to draw near. At first I saw it only indistinctly amid the flames and clouds of reddish smoke, but quickly it became clearer. It was a woman in a black veil, a slender woman with a lipless mouth and in her eyes an expression that sent icy shudders down my back. When she was standing right face to face with me, all I could see were two black, empty holes. But out of these holes the creature was nonetheless staring at me. The figure stretched out her arms toward me, and, pulled by an irresistible force, I followed her. An icy breath touched me, and I came into a world filled with faint sounds of lamentation, though there was not a person in sight.

"Then and there I asked the figure to tell me who she was. A voice answered: 'I am death.' I summoned all my strength and thought: 'I'll not follow her any more, for I want to live.' Had I betrayed this thought? In any event, she moved closer to me and put her hands on my bare breast so that I would again be under the spell of her magnetic force. I could feel her ice-cold hands on my skin, and the empty eye sockets were fixed immovably on me.

"Again I concentrated all my thoughts on living, so as to escape death in this womanly guise. Before entering the operating room, I had embraced my wife. Now the phantom of my wife came to rescue me from hell and lead me back to earthly existence.

"When Simone [his wife] appeared on the scene, the woman with the black veil departed soundlessly, on her lipless face a dreadful smile. Death could avail nothing against Simone, all radiant with youth and life. I felt only freshness and tenderness as she led me back by the hand along the same way that just before had been under the dark figure's spell.

"Gradually, gradually we left the fearful realm of shadows behind us and approached the great light. This luminousness guided us on, and finally became so bright that it began to blind me, and I had to close my eyes.

"Then suddenly a severe, dull pain set in, threatening to tear apart my chest cavity. I clutched Simone's hand harder and harder after my sudden return to consciousness.

"I found Simone sitting on my bed wearing a white nurse's uniform. I just had the strength to muster a weak smile. It was all I could do to utter one word: 'Thanks.'

"With this word I concluded a fearful but still fascinating journey into the afterworld, one I shall never forget as long as I live."

Let us suppose we have come back home a day or two after dying, that is, after we have taken a bath in infinity and eternity that has washed away all our pettiness, all the dirt. Having realized we have nothing to fear on the other side of the impenetrable rampart, who among us would be anxious to take up life again in his drear, drab dwelling?

MAURICE MAETERLINCK (1862–1949)

3

People on the Threshold

FOR THE THIRD TIME that morning, they knocked on the door of Mrs. Francis Leslie's apartment in Neuilly, near Paris. No answer. And yet they knew she was there. Something must have gone wrong. When they forced the door, they found Mrs. Leslie lifeless on the carpeted dining-room floor.

Dead! Dead beyond question.

Because Mrs. Leslie had been an American, it was decided to remove her to the nearby American Hospital in Neuilly and there officially determine the cause of her sudden demise. At the hospital there was no great hurry about examining the dead body. Around midday there was time for an autopsy. When the doctor entrusted with this task finally got around to it, he noticed, upon touching the corpse, that it was unusually warm. After all, there are definite rules for body-temperature drop—especially in cases of heart failure—and for the onset of rigor mortis and similar signs indispensable for establishing time of death.

Therefore, the doctor called in two internists, outstanding heart specialists at the hospital. The three men exchanged a look of tacit agreement. It was impossible to know, of course, whether drastically treating the body of an apparently dead person would prove successful. But at least it had to be tried.

None of the doctors involved would ever talk about the experiment if it was a failure. All they had to do was confirm the finding already registered after the preliminary examination. Meanwhile, everything would be attempted. A human life was at stake.

After the lifeless body had been laid out over an X-ray screen, skilled hands inserted a needle carrying an adrenalin injection into the right spot in the appropriate nerve plexus and then through it into the chambers of the heart.

Then they waited.

It was a long, tense wait. The injection was repeated with a stronger dosage. Then at last, suddenly, the result they had been hoping for, over gravest doubts, was there.

The dead heart began to beat. Very weakly at first, very slowly, then faster and faster, and finally with tremendous speed, wildly, desperately, like an engine being forced to the limit. But presently the heart calmed down and began to beat as regularly as most of our own hearts beat during the quiet of the night.

All this lasted for half an hour. Then the woman, who had already been certified as dead by a French doctor, opened her eyes. She looked from one to another of the three men bending over her. They watched her make a great effort to collect her thoughts, as if emerging from a great distance, and focus them at one point.

The three men said nothing, waiting for her to speak. For the first time in their lives, they were confronted by a creature who had died and come back to life.

"I was very far away. Did you call me back?"

The three doctors were at a loss. What should they say? They had merely been experimenting. Called back? Called back from where? Where had Mrs. Leslie been?

She closed her eyes, seemingly still busy straightening out her thoughts. Now two of the doctors were called away, leaving only one colleague behind to keep watch over the patient.

"Do you hear me?" the woman said. "Give me your hand. I want to feel that it's alive. I remember now, I've just been where there isn't any life. Or only another kind of life."

The young doctor left in charge of the patient pressed her waxen-soft, cool hand between his two warm, vital ones.

"Were you really there? Tell me about it—if you're not too tired. Try to speak."

And then Mrs. Leslie told about what she had experienced on the other side.

"Exactly what happened, I can't remember. But all of a sudden I was hearing a very faint, light humming sound. Or was it the colors all around me that were making the sounds? I was floating in a long shaft that seemed very narrow at first and then became wider and wider—always getting wider and with brighter and more radiant colors the farther I floated forward in the passageway.

"I know there was a dark redness above me and a dark blueness in front of me—but the higher up I looked, the lighter it became. My feet—no, I didn't have a body any more. Or did I? I had no form, anyway, that I can recall exactly.

"All of a sudden I realized I couldn't be sure what was up and what down in that tunnel, that shaftlike place.

"In any case I—or whatever I had become that made me able to float—moved forward in the tunnel. This weightlessness was wonderful.

"I heard a voice calling from far, far away. It wasn't the singing and the humming of the colors I was hearing, but a voice naming a name. I knew the voice, and I remember trying to think who it was the voice belonged to.

"As I drifted through the tunnel I couldn't identify the voice. But now I know. It was the voice of a man who died many years ago and whom I've often thought about since. Then I heard steps, as if someone was walking through a big tunnel with a loud tread. The footsteps rang out in my direction. I was in a hurry to get on ahead so I could find out who it was who was calling to me. I had to find him somewhere out there where the patch of dark blue at the far opening of this strange tunnel was getting bigger all the time. I knew that too.

"I made myself go faster. The humming became more beautiful, lighter. The colors also became clearer, and seemed to be merging together in an iridescent play of tints, only to fall apart into separate hues like a bouquet of flowers opened up. And each color had a tone. All these colors and sounds combined in a wonderful music that filled me and impelled me forward—with a feeling of unimaginable delight—toward the voice calling to me.

"And then suddenly I felt someone take hold of me. I

couldn't move ahead any more. My feet—though really I had no body—anyway, what there now was of me, striving to get out into the light, stayed rooted to the spot.

"I tried to free myself from the grip holding me from behind. But how can you loosen a hand if you have no body and even so can still be held by someone?

"Then, in the midst of sensations of bliss, I felt a pain go through me.

"When I think back on it and consider that I didn't have any physical being any more and no brain at all, I can't imagine how I could have had the feeling that someone was sticking a big steel needle downward into my head perpendicularly, right through me, as if they wanted to split me into two pieces.

"The pain got worse—while the hand gripping me got tighter and tighter—and the colors grew darker. The colors pretty soon faded out and didn't have any sound any more. And this funnel, the tunnellike place I'd been trying to work my way out of, again got narrow around me, and became so tight and small that suddenly I was terrified.

"Before, I had long gotten over being afraid, but now I was frightened and trembling. I suddenly realized I was becoming a physical person again. The hand wouldn't let me go. There was a grip like steel around my neck. The iron hand drew me back, always farther back, into a deep darkness that seemed dark red at first, but then turned into blackness, as unreal a blackness as only the eternal night can have.

"And then I was here. I heard you speaking and actually was very sad that the iron hand had brought me back. But you won't understand all this."

Mrs. Leslie said no more. She closed her eyes. Then she said, "I oughtn't have mentioned these things, never should have talked about them. Am I very sick? Do I have to stay here?"

"No, you're not terribly sick. We don't even know yet what really made you pass out. For that's all it was, a fainting fit—with tetany symptoms," the doctor said, trying to reassure the pretty lady.

"It was more than just a fainting fit. Much more than that. I was in another world, in the beyond. Definitely. So don't worry too much about me. Can you understand? I'm in a hurry to get back again. Where I was when the hand dragged me back."

The young doctor did not respond. But he noted every word so he could later turn in a precise report to the two heart specialists.

Mrs. Leslie lived on for twelve hours—exactly twelve hours. Then she died for a second time, and this time she could not be revived. An autopsy revealed a heart ailment that had resulted in cardiac failure.

"But her readiness to die was what made the difference in this woman's death. She wanted to die, perhaps because she was grieving for someone who had passed on before her."

"And this statement that she made? This description of what she experienced—as she put it—in the beyond?"

Professor A. Winstel leafed through the report which the young doctor had carefully compiled.

"Interesting—very interesting. But at the same time proof that the first death certification was incorrect. Mrs. Leslie wasn't dead. She was in a condition brought on by an unusually long stoppage of cardiac activity—which produced a tetany, a rigidity that looked like rigor mortis. A pity we didn't start the examination as soon as the dead—I mean the unconscious woman was brought in. We then might have found out that the lower jaw, where signs of rigor mortis invariably appear first, was not affected to the extent that one might have reasonably expected. This couldn't have been the case, or she couldn't have talked so quickly when she was roused from her rigid state. For it's definitely known that rigor mortis sets in first at the lower jaw, then spreads to the neck, the rump, the limbs, and eventually disappears in reverse sequence—last of all from the lower jaw.

"The report mentions her talking about strikingly beautiful colors and sounds. This is a well-known phenomenon. Visual and aural stimuli can occur in the interior of the brain without benefit of external cause. If the visual and aural centers in the brain were in an abnormal state because of a disturbance in the circulation of the blood—if a heart stoppage cut off the brain's supply of oxygen—it would be quite possible for an unconscious woman to have sensations of color and sound. This could be explained simply by a change in the oxygen supply of the brain cells.

"This has to be clearly understood, of course: The interruption of the heart action to some degree had led to a suffocation of the brain. When that happened, death would have ensued if we hadn't carried out our adrenalin experiment. We had to give it a try. After all, there was a possibility that life could be reactivated in the woman, that the dead point—dead in a double sense—could perhaps be surmounted."

"But this floating, this feeling of being carried along, this lightness in everything . . ."

"Get some heart patients to tell you about their dreams. Again and again these people have the sensation of being disembodied. In a sense they feel they are floating above themselves. And once they have achieved this apartness from their body, which they see lying below them on the ground, they have the same kind of feelings as Mrs. Leslie."

"You mean, then, this whole case, what Mrs. Leslie said, wasn't a bona fide description at all of an experience of life after death?"

"For a doctor who, day in, day out, deals with the cells, who observes their functioning, it is so very difficult to accept as true a portrayal of something in which the body and the cells play no part. If there is such a state as the 'beyond,' then I don't know whether it's even possible to tell about it."

"But she heard a voice calling to her. They just said she died because she didn't want to live, because she was yearning in her grief to be with someone."

Professor Winstel had gone to the window and was looking out into the park, where the leafless boughs of the wintry trees were lacing the sky.

"I can't say any more than that. We're dealing here with a description of a transition, a passing over, an event that very few ever get to tell about, because there is no iron hand—as they said in the report—to pull them back, if only for a matter of hours. We're dealing with a transition from here, from our world, into another one.

"It just comes to mind, too, that under certain circumstances other people besides heart patients can have similar visions—for instance, users of hashish. The fly agaric poisonous mushroom is also said to produce illusions of this type. A change in the brain's blood supply is naturally or artificially induced. This gives rise to images, colors, sounds . . ."

Professor Winstel quickly left the room.

Behind him he left on the table the report written up by the young doctor who had last conversed with Mrs. Leslie and brought to him for comment.

The doctor again thumbed through the pages. He shook his head.

"I still think it's more than just a description of a dying woman's experience of the transition from life to nothingness. It's more than that! When she was telling me about this strange business, I knew by the sound of her voice it was more."

And then he took the report and put it safely away among those records that, as a doctor, he never discussed, since they touched on the threshold between life and death that some believed they had crossed—and that others, rational and sober-minded, wanted nothing to do with.

Mrs. Leslie had floated forward in a long tunnel—toward the light.

Worthy of note is a similar deposition by a king who also claimed to have had a look into the realm of the dead. Queen Frederika of Greece kept vigil at her husband's bedside during his last hours. In her memoirs, under the heading "Experiences," she gives an impressive description of this mystical event.

Members of the Greek royal family not only scrupulously observed the outer, ceremonial forms of their religion, but were deeply religious. King Paul was filled with a genuine piety and always saw to it that he was never disturbed while at church or during his meditations. Beyond this, he had a deep sense of responsibility in regard to his duties as patron and protector of the church.

To serve as comfort for bereaved people, Queen Frederika published her personal experiences—which she called a "gift from heaven"—of those moments when the prospect of losing the family mainstay seemed unbearable.

"On Wednesday afternoon, March 4, 1964, I went into the sickroom and found Paul with a happy look on his face. I asked him how he was feeling.

"'I thought I'd already gone off,' he said softly. 'I still feel far away. It takes time to get used to being back. I must have already been on the other shore.

"'. . . I had a vision of a long dark road with a light shining at the far end. It gave a wonderful feeling of peace and happiness. A great uplift of the spirit. It's the real holy communion.

"'. . . Yes, now I understand everything. It's the truth. This is the most wonderful time of our lives.

"'. . . I like it very much there . . . There are no more problems there, only peace. When we get there everything will be straightened out. There we'll be free.'

"When Paul drew his last breath the flame of the oil-lamp (in front of a sacred icon on the island of Tinos) suddenly went out."

King Paul was one of the many among us who consciously seek the light and the truth during his days on earth. He was also one of those who have claimed they saw the goal with their own eyes after crossing the mysterious threshold.

Expressions of this longing for the "other land" are found in both the oldest and the more recent world religions.

In Roman Catholicism belief in the soul's immortality is dogma: "Whoever denies or casts in doubt the immortality of the soul, may he be anathema." And again and again allusion is made to the broad way of corruption into outermost darkness and the narrow path to paradise in eternal life.

Had anyone ever come back from the dead?

In the Christian religion the answer to this question is per-

fectly clear: Yes. Not only is the historical existence of Jesus
Christ attested on the basis of genuine documents, but the collection of happenings and episodes in the life of Jesus, his
teachings and pronouncements recorded by the four apostles
Matthew, Mark, Luke, and John, are considered to be trust-
worthy and authentic.

Many miracles are reported, greatest of which would seem
to be the resurrection following Christ's crucifixion. Jesus did
die—the fact was confirmed to Pilate by the centurion (Mark
15:44). We also read in the New Testament that three days
later the grave was empty and that Christ was seen by a number of persons. Forty days after the resurrection, as described
in Luke 24:50, came Christ's ascension into heaven, signaling
the end of the greatest personality of all history.

Was the story of Christ's return from the dead invented by
his disciples? Were his revelations just empty fantasies? Is the
same true of his otherworldly representations of heaven and
hell? (In this connection, it must be noted that it was not he
who described the "outer darkness" as an eternal abode, but
the uncompromising priests of the Middle Ages.)

Many make light of the phenomenal, dismiss it as deception
and fraud, refuse to have anything to do with it. However, in
the accounts in this book there are curious parallels to the
teachings of the world religions.

All secrets lie before us in perfect openness. Only we gradate ourselves against them, from stone to seer. There are no mysteries as such, only uninitiated of all degrees.

CHRISTIAN MORGENSTERN (1871–1914)

4

Returnee from Vietnam

A STICKY, HOT-SEASON EVENING settled down over the ravaged war zone around Chu Lai.

Jacky C. Bayne, member of the American 196th Light Infantry Brigade, serving in Vietnam, was out on a routine patrol when his tracking dog stepped on a mine.

The doctors in the nearest field hospital worked for almost an hour to bring J. C. Bayne back to life with artificial respiration and heart massage. No use—the cardiograph showed no sign of heart action. The soldier had died of his severe wounds —the typical tragic ending, it appeared, to the story of many in Vietnam. But for Bayne it proved to be only the beginning of his "second life."

The corpse lay for some hours in a death-registration unit before an embalmer got around to it. He began his work by laying open the upper femoral artery so that the embalming fluid could be pumped in.

To the embalmer's astonishment, the artery showed a very weak pulse. Bayne was rushed back to the field hospital at top speed. A second resuscitation effort was made. Finally, a massive transfusion of blood brought the success no one had dared hope for. The clinically dead Jacky Bayne was revived, to be flown back much later to the United States for further treatment at Walter Reed Hospital.

So far he has never talked about what he felt and experienced during the time he was clinically dead. To this day he has refused to make any statement on what it was like, saying: "The good Lord brought me back from Vietnam. What I saw on the other side—that's my big secret."

Yet the psychiatrists are convinced that in the course of

years they will succeed, perhaps by using hypnotic means, in luring out of him what he has so far held back. Sensational disclosures are expected.

Still under rehabilitation treatment, he has begun to have more powerful and vivid dreams, which can be detected by his REMs (rapid eye movements) during sleep. Often, while asleep, he talks about long corridors and a shining light.

From the few details that have gradually leaked out, it can be assumed that Jacky Bayne's brain, because of the long cut-off of oxygen, suffered an irreparable insult that presumably damaged the speech center. In this regard one generally goes by the findings of resuscitative medicine, according to which ten minutes is the upper limit of tolerance in an interruption of the cerebral blood supply. After this the brain cells begin to deteriorate, and the deterioration cannot be reversed.

However, this rule-of-thumb limit is no longer 100 percent valid, according to recent research. The boundary between life and death seems to have been displaced now that a Cologne brain researcher has published his investigative results.

University docent Dr. Konstantin Hossmann, working under the direction of Professor Klaus Zülch at the Max Planck Institute of Brain Research, discovered, after a long series of experiments with apes and cats, that the brain can be revived even as much as an hour after so-called extinction. According to his tests, the brain cells do not really die during such periods of deprivation; rather, the blood vessels in the brain contract. If blood should begin to flow again, these blood vessels remain shrunken. To expand them, Dr. Hossmann pumped in arterial blood under high pressure. Measurable signs of life then returned to the brain cells.

Since heart action and circulation of the blood can often be restored in victims of accidents or infarction, the Hossmann procedure for revitalizing brain function takes on great significance.

In the case of Jacky Bayne, the military doctors have been almost painfully conventional about meeting their obligation to preserve confidentiality. They merely label the case a medical rarity.

However, this question arises: If these experienced internists did not expand the shrunken cells by artificial shock, is it not possible that the body did the same on its own? This question has to remain open.

The ancient Egyptians do not seem to have overlooked the second possibility.

Mute witnesses, departed thousands of years ago, still exist to testify to Egyptian experiments to awaken the dead to a "second life," experiments that, of course, differed from the methods used today in resuscitation. In Aniba, south of Aswan, a mummy dating back four thousand years offers evidence that in thought and deed the priests and physicians of that age attempted to help people back to life.

We know how passionately the ancient Egyptians clung to life and all its pleasures. If they gave a great deal of thought to death, they did so only to outwit it and escape from its dominion. And if they never succeeded in that, at least they used every magical means to ensure that the deceased's sojourn in the beyond approximated his life on earth.

It is understandable that the comprehensive literature of the dead originally intended exclusively for the Pharaohs, their confidants, and priests—the magic texts which we can read today as formulated in the *Book of the Dead*—has become popularly accessible.

The pyramids over the Pharaohs' burial chambers and the mummification of the dead by no means signified finality to the Egyptians. In the Cairo museum of antiquities, there are documents with over two hundred lines of hieroglyphs as well as nearly fifty papyrus scrolls yielding information on Egyptian methods of trying to bring people back to life. These fragments reveal that there were conflicting views on the subject among physicians and priests.

The oldest relevant reports concern the experiments of the physician Olei En-ches, who lived at about 2,500 B.C.

After the body had been propped up in a frame, herbs and wonder-working plants were placed on the body and rubbed into the skin so the body would be anointed by their juices.

These restorative measures were kept up for nine days, at the end of which, if they were then deemed ineffective, embalming was begun.

About a century later—during the Eighteenth Dynasty—an attempt to reform the ancient Egyptian state religion in general failed, but thereafter the primitive revival ceremony was replaced by another procedure for "returning the soul to a new body."

When a high official felt that death was drawing nigh, of his own volition he could commit himself to a procedure in which blood was drained from his arteries and organs. After his carotid artery had been slit open, of course, the dying man passed out and felt no more as blood was sucked from him through a number of tubes with the help of a suction device. Death's candidate expired in the belief that new life could be generated in him after this torture by immediately having "blood-building plant juice" pumped into his veins.

After long controversy between the priests and the imperial physician Sandruval, the priests succeeded in having Sandruval declared guilty of instigating and practicing sacrilege on the dead. He was walled up alive, though not without being provided with a pitcher of his "life juice" and his sucking machine to use with it.

It was Ramses III (c. 1,250 B.C.) who first issued an edict strictly forbidding all restorative experiments on both mummies and the recently dead, and thereafter this sacrilegious form of "blood washing" could no longer develop in Egyptian medicine.

Priestly consultation during medical experiments was also brought to an end. In spite of this, the idea of "bringing the dead back to life" was never completely abolished among learned men until the fall of ancient Egypt.

The fervid interest of the ancient Egyptians in the mysteries of death was not impaired by the failure to effect a visible revival of the dead.

On the basis of a comprehensive literature of the dead, we know that at one time only the Pharaohs and high dignitaries had the privilege of arranging their stay in eternity. But a social or religious revolution ensued (however it may be characterized in traditional terms, it brings to mind the Communist movement), and after that everybody gained the right to know about the religious mysteries. Thenceforth, any ordinary mortal could be the equal of a king, who earlier had alone been privy to the *Book of the Dead* to serve as his pilgrim's guide through the stations of the underworld.

Instructed by revelations and visions, the priests had compiled a great deal of lore about life after death. This knowledge served to counsel the soul after death. Now the magic texts found in the burial chambers of the mighty after their downfall could be studied by any living mortal while still alive, enabling him, too, to prepare for life after death.

The Egyptian *Book of the Dead* throws light on a belief in the development of the spirit by steps. Pilgrim staff in hand, the souls of the dead set out on the long road leading to the fields of Osiris, a road in the region of the Milky Way, thought of as the Great White Nile of heaven. At the highest stage the Creator is confronted.

Actually, there were two essences or souls, the *ka* and the *ba*. The *ka* seems to have been conceived of as a delicate physical substance, a corporeal genius or double, whereas the *ba* was pure soul or spirit. Symbolizing the *ba*'s ability for free and untrammeled flight, it was represented as a bird with a human head. It is often pictured crouched over the entrance to a tomb, or in flight down to the embalmed corpse.

There were many incantations to be spoken on the day of burial, at that time when the soul, separated from the body, departs into the afterworld. The departed soul resorts first to the divine spirits that lead purified *ba* to the sacred precincts of Osiris. Careful study of the magic incantations shows there were many interruptions and stayovers on the pilgrimage through the underworld to the luminous heights.

Khu, as the transfigured soul or intelligence was called, was pursued by frightful monsters and armed spirits. To help them withstand these trials and perils, at burial the dead were provided with a number of amulets. Incense and prayers above the crown of flowers decking the head of the deceased were also part of the interment ceremony. A likeness of the scarab beetle, sacred symbol of the sun-god Khepera, was hung about the dead man's neck in the form of a gem, or laid on the mummy's breast as a stone carving. This talisman was supposed to repel crocodile-headed spirits, snake demons, wild animals, and the like.

The incantations and exorcisms were written in the first person. Thus, in the *Book of the Dead:*

> Make way, grotesque crocodile demon Sui!
> Truly, you have no power over me!
> For, a sanctified spirit, I live and change
> Through the magic strength of words in me.

Or, again:

> Back, Zerek [a demon],
> Back, you snakeheaded demon!
> The gods Geb and Shu bar the way.
> You may not touch me! Stay where you are!
>
> Be prudent then: With foul-smelling rats
> You feed yourself, which are hated by Ra;
> And you gnaw the bones
> Of a rotting cat.

The dead person tarried in all regions of the beyond, saying prayers and litanies, undergoing all sorts of metamorphoses. He emerged as a divine personality who, far from beseeching the gods for mercy, demanded their assistance, just as he had commanded all dangerous presences to keep their distance.

> I am the great despot, master of the sword.
> Rise not up against me, I am Set!
> Touch me not! I am Horus!

At the end of the journey, in the sacred hall where the godhead rules amid a sort of court of jurymen gods, the soul again speaks out, saying:

"I come here to gaze upon the gods, the great ones.

"And, tasting the heavenly bread, to take possession of eternal life. I have made my way to the last bounds of heaven, where Osiris, the divine soul, reigns."

In many of the records set down by Egyptian priests there are striking similarities to the burial rites of the Roman Catholic Church.

❧⅊❧

The spirit choir around him seeming
New to himself, he scarce divines
His heritage of newborn Being,
When like the Holy Host he shines.
Behold how he each band hath cloven,
The earthly life around him thrown,
And through his garb of ether woven
The early force of youth is shown!
Vouchsafe to me that I instruct him!
Still dazzles him the Day's new glare.

JOHANN WOLFGANG VON GOETHE (1749–1832),
Faust (translated by Bayard Taylor)

5

Sealed Lips

THE LIPS OF THOSE who know too much are closed as if with
seven seals. No one presumes to break these seals to make the
mute speak.

Victor Cleave kept silent for three years. Cleave earlier had
been a railroad employee in Folkestone, a Kentish town on
the Strait of Dover. As a souvenir of his railroad employment,
he had a deep scar on the upper parietal bone left by a severe
head injury sustained many years before. For a long time he
had had no more headaches. Then suddenly he was overcome
by a growing fatigue. One Wednesday evening he fell asleep
at supper, was helped to bed by his wife—and did not wake up
until four years later. Asleep, he at first breathed normally, but
later ever more weakly, until he was breathing so feebly that
the doctors expected his heart to stop at any moment. In all
events, his respiration was so shallow that his body clearly was
not getting enough oxygen.

"Naturally, we were able to feed him artificially. We could
massage him. We were also able to prevent muscular atrophy,
so that he stayed at more or less the same weight. In addition,
we had to make sure that his body temperature was kept at a
normal 98.6°. Otherwise he would have died. The tissue cannot tolerate continuous supercooling."

These were the only measures used by the doctors in caring
for Victor Cleave. After all, they had no serious hopes of being
able to save him. To outward view, he looked like a person
stricken by a severe attack of sleeping sickness. But all the
appropriate therapy usually followed in such cases failed to
work with Cleave.

He simply lay there and slept. His wife got used to his condition and spent day and night with her husband. The doctors
had told her he would go any day. But she no longer believed
he would die, at least after the first two years. He kept right on
sleeping, and in sleep looked well so long as his body temperature was maintained.

After four years of this had passed, the wife noticed that her
husband's eyelids were beginning to flutter. Then, one day, he
opened his eyes. He had no idea where or who he was. He had
even forgotten his wife's name. When she brought their two
children to the bedside, he asked her who they were. He had
forgotten he had two children.

Gradually they led him back into life and to all the activities
that go with it—including reading, writing, and speaking in-
telligibly. When he had reached that point in his recovery, a
well-known clergyman interested in psychological studies
came to Cleave and asked him to talk about what he had experienced during his four years of sleep. Cleave shook his head
mistrustfully and refused to answer. The clergyman insisted,
relying on his influence as a spiritual adviser and psychological
investigator.

Finally Cleave did decide to talk. What he related was a most
interesting recital coming as it did from a person who had
been completely out of touch with the world for years.

"At the start it was very hard for me to get used to being in
this world again. I've never told a soul before what I went
through and saw. And if you hadn't insisted, if you hadn't said
you're sort of standing in for a higher power on earth, I
wouldn't be telling you anything, either. But maybe somebody
has to know about it. In certain situations it could be important to you and other people. But never mention me by name
when you talk about it. For if I had my way . . .

"If it just depended on me, I'd close my eyes this minute
and go to sleep again. If you want the truth of it—there's nothing in this world to hold me.

"I don't know whether I was really on the other side, or just
dreaming that I was.

"Anyway, I was in a land where there were flowers and

trees I've never seen on earth and never heard of in other countries.

"It was a land where there were living beings who had a fantastic ability to build palaces and houses with big, heavy columns—palaces and high-rise buildings—shaped in forms people have never thought of here. At the beginning, after I woke up, I tried to draw these buildings on paper. But I couldn't do it. When I'd start to draw and try to translate them into the dimensions of length and breadth and depth, everything would blur together, and all I'd get was some ridiculous earth-type structure—not at all like what I'd seen.

"So, then, I lived in this world of tall buildings and columns. There were many creatures all around me. I believe we all were shaped very much like people here on earth. Yet it has been the same with them as with sketching the buildings. I simply haven't been able to do it. When I shut my eyes, I still pretty much remember what I and the others were like. But if I try to represent them when I open my eyes, materialize them with strokes and lines and circles on paper, then all of a sudden I'm stuck.

"My conceptions just aren't adequate.

"But was I really like a person, the way I am today? I remember that the beings who were with me could walk right through things. At first that struck me as astonishing, unbelievable. Which of course it was. And yet, the more I think back on it, the more certain I am that I, myself, could also walk through buildings and columns—if I wanted to.

"I know what I've just said is nonsense. It could be I only dreamed everything. But did anyone ever dream anything like that? Today, if I can believe the calendar, I had four years of time in that other world.

"Yes, it strikes me now that out there I didn't have any sense of time, in that existence among columns and buildings and creatures who were so strong they could lift and move anything. Time didn't seem to exist there.

"Without anybody ever speaking to me—for nobody ever said anything out loud in this world, they just thought what they wanted to say and the other person knew what it was—I had a notion while I was there that I was in a time of waiting, a kind of probationary period.

"Every new arrival knows or feels his waiting period. That's what I believe, anyway. Perhaps my being able to walk right through buildings and columns had something to do with this waiting period. For there were others who could control and give shape to matter out there . . .

"Once something happened that is the unclearest part of my experience during these four years. I suddenly sank into the ground as if a trapdoor had opened under me. I heard a muffled howling sound that became steadily louder and more distinct, and the more this howling and humming grew in my ears, the more I got a vague idea that a door that just previously had stood open had now closed behind me. Yet I didn't even question why this should be so.

"From that point until I woke up again here in my bed was the worst part of it all. I felt as if I didn't belong to my body any more, my own carcass. I seemed to be here on earth only on leave.

"But of course I'm on leave!

"I'm not here for always—not for long. I don't know, either, why I had to come back here at all and relearn everything I'd forgotten. I came back to earth with a brain that had everything erased from it by having lived in the other world.

"But was it really the other world? Or was it just a preliminary to it, a waiting period, a period of purification—as I sometimes suppose today.

"I don't know exactly, and nobody can know. But the most awful thing for me is my disappointment when again and again I struggle to sketch the buildings and what I saw over there, draw them on paper. And what always comes of it? A ridiculous, flat picture, just like what you'd see on earth—whereas out there everything seemed to live and breathe—a rhythm I first began to be aware of when I had to come back, on leave, to earth . . ."

In the interpretation of what Cleave experienced during his four years of sleep, it becomes apparent that anyone reaching into our world from the beyond knows no obstacles. The armored walls of the deepest vaults no longer exist for him. He penetrates them in the same way as did the creatures that Cleave believed he saw walking right through otherwise solid objects.

Some day we shall know more about what happens between these worlds. And when this occurs, we shall be knocking on the door that—perhaps only for the transitional or waiting period that Victor Cleave told about—separates us from the world beyond the grave. In this special case the brain specialists will be quick to object that Cleave had suffered a head injury that left not only the skull but the brain itself badly scarred. It is known that brain scars can give rise to pressures that have a strong stimulant effect. Consequently, the specialist will try to determine whether, because of previous brain damage, there was pressure on the sleep center and on certain zones of the cortex. The specialist dealing with brain trauma has much the same point of view as the famous Greek physician Hippocrates, who thousands of years ago said that mental illness is explicable only in terms of the brain and the human organism.

The brain specialist will first of all try to view Cleave's experiences as a protracted dream. Having done this much, he will then have only one more puzzle to solve: How did Cleave's fixed ideas reach his subconscious to develop there? For even if a brain disturbance is assumed to have been the cause and source of the continuous dream, the prerequisites for further organization of the dream had to be much the same as in a normal dream experience.

In such case, somewhere and somehow Cleave must have already heard or read about or at least wished for the things he described as having seen in his dream.

But Cleave contends this was not so. He claims that all his life he was a very stable man who "as a rule never dreamed at all."

Over and beyond this, parapsychology comes into the picture. Parapsychology assures us that a purely biological interpretation—that brain-cell function alone is the determinant, that only the memories stored in the cortical layers can give rise to dreams—simply is not enough to account for all the things Cleave slowly recounted when he finally decided to break his silence.

All over the world, in Germany and Holland, in France and South America, in Australia and the Indies, there have been opportunities to observe similar cases of people who fall into a deathlike sleep, but who have not died, but lived again. And who, for the most part, have not talked about what it was like during their long absence, or, if they did talk, told stories that were quite different from Cleave's.

The most remarkable thing, and at the same time the most unsettling, is the fact that all these accounts are different. The seeker finds it impossible to find the least thread of uniformity in the welter of reports, long or short, the confessions laboriously extracted, word by word, from people who have come back to earth on leave.

However, in our search for additional material, those who have dealt with the representations of mystics point out that the visions of innumerable people—visions that the mystics themselves say arose through concentration, or through the practice of old or modern yoga—do in fact agree with some of the accounts of the kind just described. Parallels appear where none would be expected.

But now, of course, the skeptic steps forward and points out that people who deliberately venture into such spheres obviously will have read everything by others in the same field. The brain quickly absorbs everything touching important centers of active interest, as surely as a blotter, a mirror. Therefore, it does not take much for the memory to register the accounts of others and then, one day when conditions are right, give them back from its store. When this happens, parallels come into being, leading to amazed announcements that uniform descriptions of the afterworld do exist. We see that the skeptical critic is not to be shaken from his point of view. He will not yield or admit anything unless he is forced to do it without qualification.

Perhaps it is better this way—in the interest of research and neutral testing. Such animadversions will often be useful in ensuring that sharply discriminating criteria are employed in the collection of similar reports. The chaff must be separated from the wheat; illusions arising from a brain responding to pathological stimuli must be separated from spontaneous deep experiences.

Besides the doubters who, in their exaggerated objectivity, seize on the least opportunity to contradict, there are still others: the specialists who are in a position to actually see the point at which being and not-being meet. These are the heart and brain surgeons, who are the most apt to break the seven seals closing secretive lips.

᪥

Although every human is subject to death, yet everyone wants to escape it. Indeed, to human beings death is what water is to fire, its archenemy. Whence does it stem, the powerful longing, this enormous craving, this unslakable thirst for deathlessness? It is a feeling that death is completely unsuitable for us, and with it a feeling that a deathless state must be possible. This feeling is just as strong—and therefore overpowering—as the impulse out of which it is born, the impulse to escape death, that is, it is as strong as the dread of dying; consequently, the content of the primeval feeling generated by the fear of death is as follows: The condition of mortality is inappropriate for you; the only thing suitable for you is im-mortality, the state in which you can no longer die. Or, in short: Death is contrary to your nature.

GEORG GRIMM (1868–1945)

6

Death on Call

"I CAN'T DIE RIGHT NOW!

"If I have a heart attack today or tomorrow, you've got to revive me no matter what. My son is on his way here now. I have some important things to tell him. I should have done it before. But I thought there would still be time. The existence of the whole plant, the jobs of thousands of workers, all my plans for the future—everything depends on it. But they tell me he can't get here until the day after tomorrow. And I don't know whether I'll still be living then. Ever since this morning I've been feeling so weak, so miserable. That's why I had them call you.

"Dr. Hyman, you're the only man on earth I know who can artificially prolong a person's life—at least for hours—though perhaps for days. That's all I want from you."

The seventy-eight-year-old American millionaire, Philip L., lay back exhausted on the pillows and looked anxiously to see how Dr. Hyman would respond.

"Relax, take it easy. You had me called in. I'm at your service. I'll do everything in my power. You'll see your son."

A smile of relief crossed the millionaire's face. Dr. Hyman turned the situation back to the doctor who up to now had been in charge of the case, and they retired to an anteroom. Everything was carefully agreed on.

"Let things run their course to the finish. Alert me the moment you think death has arrived. Then I'll see what I can do."

The regular physician looked a little skeptically at Hyman, now unpacking his equipment in the anteroom to have everything ready for the decisive moment. And it could come at any second.

"Please come, Doctor. He's having another heart attack."

"It won't be long before it's his last one," the doctor muttered as he went into the sickroom. Indeed, the patient was unconscious by the time he reached the bedside. A few seconds later he took the patient's pulse, listened to his heart, examined his eye reflexes, and then held off for a moment, watching closely. The patient was already past his agony and gone into the realm of death. The doctor turned to the people standing about the bed and said:

"The patient has just expired. This is my official finding."

He packed his small doctor's bag, wrote out a death certificate, and left, while Dr. Hyman, helped by an assistant, was beginning his interesting task. His intention was to restore to life—for a short interval—a man who had been officially declared extinct, to revive him to a point at which he would be able to think and make decisions as in ordinary life.

The apparatus Dr. Hyman had brought with him was quickly arranged on a table brought in for the occasion. After some rapid probing, Hyman sank four long needles into the area of the body where the heart was located. He then sent weak electric currents into the heart, knowing that by this means he could get the heart muscle to contract. He listened attentively. After half a minute he detected a weak heartbeat. Soon the beat grew stronger. However, six hours passed before the millionaire opened his eyes again. About fifteen minutes after awakening from death, he tried, in a very weak voice, yet calmly and sensibly, to speak a few words.

"No word yet of my son? . . . Thank you, Dr. Hyman. You must keep this apparatus going till he's here."

The patient lay back on his pillows, listening to his artificially sustained heartbeat. He may also have been thinking about what he had seen and experienced during his deathly interlude.

After some three hours had gone by, he signaled Hyman to come closer. "I'd like to tell you what I just went through," he said. "Send the other people away.

"I found myself," he went on, "in a great white place lit up by a sun so strong I couldn't bear to look at it. At first I was all by myself. Then I saw other people in the distance—or at least something that was moving. I shouted and waved, and I had the feeling they were waving back. But whoever they were out there, they couldn't come close to me. I suddenly had the feeling I was two people. I looked down and saw my arms at my sides, and yet at the same time it seemed to me I was waving.

"When I started off toward the others, the way to them grew longer. Then I gave up. I suddenly realized I could never get to the others, that I had a long, long time ahead of me.

"The sun shining down on this white place turned somewhat reddish and murky. Somehow this color felt good to my eyes. And when I set out to walk, I saw my legs were just hanging there, quite motionless, like my arms. Someone other than myself seemed to be carrying out my movement. I cudgeled my mind trying to figure out this phenomenon.

"I also saw—really the only figure I made out clearly—I saw a woman, who, I realized, was my wife, dead twenty years ago. She was among the people beckoning to me. I was overjoyed at seeing her so quickly. But then I realized it wasn't possible to be with her at once after all and that I still had a long way to go.

"I strode on but presently found myself going backward, even while those amazing legs I've just told you about—the ones that were giving me, or some second me, the power of locomotion—kept right on going forward. I think, Doctor, this happened at the moment when you brought me back.

"Check again, will you, to see if there's any word of my son."

Dr. Hyman knew it would take at least sixteen hours for the son to arrive. Any sooner was impossible. Again and again he looked anxiously at his apparatus, working away industriously on the little table, at regular intervals shooting electric currents into a heart that had already died once.

The apparatus was kept going for exactly twenty-four hours, thirty minutes, and ten seconds. The millionaire's son arrived on schedule. Again Dr. Hyman checked his machine. Everything was in order. There would be no breakdown. He left the room so the dying man could impart to his son in private the instructions that had seemed so important to him that he could not think of dying before passing them along.

It took only a few minutes, after which the son came out and said in a whisper:

"You can go in, Dr. Hyman. My father's asking for you."

"You're a wonderful man, Dr. Hyman. I've talked everything over with my boy. Everything's in order now. I'd like to be able to have a few moments' sleep. But the throbbing of that machine bothers me. The current feels as if it's going right into my head. Turn it off for half an hour, please."

Dr. Hyman took another close look at the millionaire, rapidly weighed the pros and cons, and then did turn the current off, so the exhausted man could sleep. He knew, of course, that cutting off the current would spell the end. But it had been a hopeless undertaking to begin with, outwitting death. The machine's artificial pulse could not maintain life indefinitely. Eventually the man who had already been "out there" would have to go back when the great weariness came over him. And this seemed to be happening now.

A second later the heartbeat stopped. The patient slumped —and this time was dead for good.

Dr. Albert Hyman has often discussed this and other experimental experiences at American medical congresses. For many years he has been working with a method of restoring the heartbeat by the introduction of electric currents directly into the heart and coronary vessels. He claims that a more or less normal circulation can be produced in an ostensibly dead heart and certainly in one that is moribund.

"I have carried out five hundred animal experiments, all of them with good results. In my original experiments I inserted a needle exactly between the two upper chambers of the heart and then introduced an electric current at certain rhythmic intervals to stimulate the normal heartbeat.

"If a heart has stopped as the result of overexertion, or because of physical or electric shock, I can start it beating again.

But all such resuscitative methods fail if the heart has become too rigid and hard. In other words, if the intervention comes too late.

"I'm fully aware I can never banish death from the world by this method. I realize I cannot keep a dying person alive for a long period. But in many cases it's a question of just a few more minutes or hours, enough time to get things done that can have the greatest importance for the dying person's associates and for the world at large."

Dr. Hyman was developing his procedure at about the same time Professor Smirnow in Moscow was attempting to bring heart-attack victims back to life, at least for a time. In several cases, particularly in cases of death by shock, the period of reprieve lasted for some time.

One of the most interesting cases of this type occurred in Brooklyn, New York. The wife of a businessman named Redino lost consciousness and was declared dead after being taken to a nearby hospital. All the characteristic death signs that appear a few minutes after a patient has expired were duly noted. The two doctors who made the determination were about to leave the room when a nurse suddenly cried: "She just sighed. I heard her clearly!"

"Impossible. She must have still had some air in her lungs. After all, rigor mortis begins in the jaws. It could have stretched the throat muscles and vocal cords."

"No, she really sighed—just like a person sighs who is in pain."

"Quick, then, get the Hyman apparatus."

Before the heart had had time to harden, the currents were sent pulsing through the critical organ.

After a few minutes artificial breathing was also supplied. Oxygen was pumped into the lungs.

After an effort that lasted for three hours, Amalie Redino was again conscious. She felt very weak and had to have nurses in attendance day and night. But she lived.

"It was wonderful. I saw a sky over me that was bluer than anything I'd ever seen on earth. I met people I hadn't seen for a long time. I had a marvelous feeling of well-being, indescribable. I floated in this endless blueness above me. And the higher I got, the more the clouds turned violet. I heard wonderful music coming from far off, and I seemed to soar on its waves. I felt so light, so happy.

"But then I suddenly remembered my two little daughters. I was afraid the children wouldn't be brought up the way I would do it if I had enough time left to arrange everything. I worried about the children and wanted to get back to them. Someone told me it would be very painful to go back—much more painful than just disappearing into where I was. You see, going out into that rapturous blueness with the violet clouds wasn't painful a bit. It was so easy and simple.

"And now they said going back would be painful. I hesitated.

"But thinking about the two children disturbed all my inner peace and feeling of happiness. I knew I had to go back.

"So there I was, with the clouds sinking down, making myself get heavier just by willing it, until suddenly here I was again.

"Would you call my sister? I've got to tell her everything I want for the children. Get her quick, for I don't think I can stay here very long. I'm only here for a few hours."

But this Italian mother lived on for three weeks. It was not until the third week after her reawakening from death by heart failure that she definitively expired. This was the most interesting experiment with the Hyman apparatus.

Many may wonder whether the mechanism of death can be outwitted, even for hours, with just the introduction of electric currents into the heart, simply by the electrical stimulation of certain nerve ganglia in the cardiac region. But it is a fact that death practically always proceeds from the heart and that heart stoppage is the first sign of somatic death. As long as the heart is beating, a person is alive. This is true whatever other organic breakdowns there may be. Stoppage of the heart is the phenomenon that introduces death, in a sense signals the end, even though cardiac arrest can of course be the end result of other events.

But if death spreads out from the heart, so to speak, the

stoppage of the heart itself must be caused by something. And the root cause is found in the central nervous system. The paralysis of movement centers, which are in the medulla oblongata, or the excitation of inhibiting centers in the control mechanism, which can be occasioned by a brain injury or by reflex action, can suffice to influence the cardiac controls so that death ensues.

We have seen how the heart surgeon, skillfully using artificial means, can delay death by hours. The day is not far off when, using similar but even more sophisticated devices, it will be possible to overcome paralysis in the movement centers of the medulla oblongata, that is, the lower or posterior part of the brain where respiration, circulation, swallowing, and other functions are regulated. But even in this age of lobotomy and brain surgery, injecting into the brain is a risky business; mastering it to the extent needed to banish death can be done only gradually.

In many cases death occurs because the heart is brought to a standstill by psychic shocks, acting through the neural channels just described. These shocks may actually be insignificant as such. But if exaggerated and potentiated by mental sickness, as in the case of people suffering from hallucinations, they can result in death.

There are many crude examples to show that stress states can lead to sickness and death. Stress arising from the fear of old age, or from family or professional worries, sometimes gives rise to psychic conflicts that the victim feels are too much for him to cope with. Thus he flees into sickness, at the end of which stands a "death wish," so to speak. This psychogenic type of death is essentially different in motivation and deed from suicide.

Fatal heart attacks and infarctions, asthma attacks, and the like in some cases may suddenly appear. Death may intervene after a successful operation, at a time when, from the medical point of view, all danger is past. The cause for this can be explained only in terms of powerful emotions.

Psychogenic death brought on by despair, self-denigration, feelings of anxiety, and guilt complexes is by no means a rarity.

In any case, in brain surgery there are already a number of operating procedures in the planning stage—and tried out so far only on animals—the end purpose of which is, under certain conditions, to outmaneuver death and deny him his prey for an interval.

Isolated cases of recoveries of this sort have already been achieved. One patient suffering from pathological hyper-reactivity in the central nervous system began to suffer the usual psychological side effects. He began to see failure in the exhausting perspectives of despair and pessimism. Whereas the healthy person looks at the future in the light of the past, the psychologically sick person sees it only in a perspective that he supplies with rich fantasy.

In cases like this, if certain connections in the brain can be severed successfully, the picture changes immediately. The depressed person who, because of exceedingly strong affect, feels himself, in his unreal world, to be perishing in a slough of despond, quickly becomes sound again and able to resume his place in normal life.

"They told me later I had a stroke. All that I remember is that suddenly I felt a bright beam of light going through me. This beam of light was accompanied by a stabbing pain. But when this pain—it was around the heart—faded out, everything was beautiful and peaceful.

"I was floating in a world that I had never imagined I would see again during the terrible nightmares of earlier weeks: a world of light and soothing bliss, which filled my whole being from within outward. The ghosts, the black figures, which at the beginning threatened to come and get me, no longer had any power over me. I knew they were still lurking somewhere, somewhere in the distance. But I knew, too, they would never reach me again—never!"

The foregoing comes from a man who had sunk into a deep coma. An ad hoc attempt was made to save him by a daring entry into the brain while simultaneously resuscitation was applied to the heart. The operation was carried out in masterful fashion and succeeded. This time death was cheated. The cause of the trouble was removed. The patient, whose heart had nearly stopped from dread and terror—these emotions arising from imagined causes—was able to return to a normal existence once the techniques of modern brain surgery had been successfully applied in a last-ditch effort.

Happy will they be who lend an ear to
the words of the dead.

LEONARDO DA VINCI (1452–1519)

7

Souls Ill at Ease

"YOU MUST AVENGE ME!

"I'm not able to get free of the earth. I'm waiting for deliverance. I was taken too soon from this world—much too soon. Now I'm faring like all who die too young through violence.

"We cannot find peace. We go about and are very close to you. We are near you because we still feel connected with you, and we call on you to speak to us or help us. You can help us—who died too early and in truth are not yet free and must wander about for a long time.

"Any one of us who wishes to, who considers it right to do so and who still has something owing from you, he is allowed to speak with you—as I am speaking.

"Yes, you must avenge me! For the man who killed me is still going around free. And as long as he is free and on the lookout for other victims, as long as he is not in solitary confinement or sent to his death, I must come night after night and beg you to avenge me!"

This was the story that an old man living near Toulon, which is on the Mediterranean coast of France, brought to the police.

They gave him a searching look and put him down as a lunatic. Still, when he wasn't telling about his alleged nightly visitations, he was the most sensible, down-to-earth fellow in the world.

"My daughter demands atonement for her violent death. You know the case of little Juliette Maçon. Don't you remember? A year ago my daughter was murdered. She died a terrible death—assaulted, raped, and strangled. We buried her. But that's not the end of it. My daughter comes to me night after night and pleads with me to avenge her.

"Do you expect me to go out looking for the murderer? Isn't that your job? Aren't you paid out of taxes to track down murderers? Free me from these dreams in which my daughter speaks to me, tells me about this other world where she is and where she can find no peace.

"Could you put up with it if you were I? Seeing your own daughter night after night in dreams, standing in front of you all pale, stretching out her white hands, hands with no blood in them any more, all the while sobbing and pleading:

"'Avenge me, you must avenge me.'

"That's why I'm here again. Before you've always shrugged your shoulders and sent me away. But now I can't stand it any more. If you're going to keep on treating me like this and letting the murderer go free, I'd rather go and be with my daughter. Then I'll be among those who died too young and because of that can find no peace."

But again they dismissed the old man, with some words of consolation. They also spoke with the court doctor and the police specialist for the mentally deranged.

"This man is the querulous type of psychopath. He has taken up spiritualism and necromancy. All this may have unsettled him. And this business about the souls of those who have died too young and are unable to find peace accords exactly with what a spiritist community, some time ago, gave out as an explanation for a great number of inexplicable phenomena reported here and there in a variety of places throughout France."

With this the case was closed for the police.

The tormented father, however, still firmly believes that the figure appearing to him in his dreams really is his daughter, and that she claims she will find deliverance only when avenged.

This case is cited because it is important in studying reports on the beyond to become acquainted with testimony, authentic or alleged, represented as coming from third persons in the afterworld, as when the young girl appeared to her father.

The Metaphysical Society of Amiens, France, had a similar case actually put to test, after the medium Jean Lenoble repeatedly saw a woman who had been shot to death—or so she said. The woman had Mongol features. Lenoble had no idea why the woman should have chosen only him to tell her devastating story to in his dreams:

"In a few days I shall tell you my name.

"It's a man's name because I only look like a woman, and I was shot as a woman. I have Mongolian blood. I came to France for a definite purpose and was supposed to find out something. But I was trapped in an ambush, and they misunderstood what it was I wanted and what I was supposed to do. And before I could clear myself, I was condemned and shot, during the troubled days of November, 1943. I was buried under a big tree. I can tell you the place exactly. But listen carefully:

"You must go to this place and dig me up. You must determine what actually happened at my death. For the one who murdered me must pay for the deed. . . .

"I come to you because you are able to hear me. It's not easy for us, from the world in which I speak, to find a spokesman everyone can understand, someone to be interpreter for me.

"Follow my instructions. You will find everything borne out. Until the world knows what happened to me, I shall suffer very much. I know that, because I died, a second murder was perpetrated. My murder started a chain of them. You must help break this chain."

So went the report given by the medium Jean Lenoble to the Amiens Metaphysical Society.

Lenoble's bill of particulars was checked out. A skeleton actually was found on the site he had named. Inquiry established the date of the mysterious shooting. Is this valid proof that Lenoble did in fact converse with a dead person in the afterworld?

Cautious specialists in metaphysical investigation point out that Lenoble could have learned by chance about the execution and the place where the corpse was secretly buried, as well as all the circumstances surrounding the affair. But whether he used previous knowledge deliberately to construct an interesting case, or whether things he had once known came back to him in his trance—this is a question that must be settled elsewhere.

The similarity of recitals having to do with beings who die too young and then can find no rest was taken by itself as almost proof enough for rejecting Lenoble's story. In fact, it was done using almost the same words as the Toulon doctor when he pointed out that once such notions arise in circles interested in spiritism and begin to circulate, they become common coin among everyone who believes in such things.

"Last night I saw Margaret. She came to me and told me everything. She had a big, gaping wound on her neck. She said to me:

"'If I were alive, I wouldn't be able to talk with this wound. You can see—my throat is practically severed.

"'They keep telling me, the ones where I am now, to talk to someone on the other side so that there will be atonement for the deed done to me. It was Ernest Foutch. I can tell you exactly how it happened.

"'You remember how I was celebrating my fourteenth birthday with my girlfriends. Late in the evening I walked one of them a piece down the road to see she got home. Ernest Foutch must have seen me. He'd often had an eye on me before. On my way back—I was all alone in the dark—suddenly Ernest Foutch jumped me. He pulled me to the ground by my hair. He tried to kiss me, and then he bit me in the throat. But his hands kept ripping at my hair.

"'He bent my head back, always pulling harder on my hair, and then he stuck a knife into my neck with his left hand. At this moment I couldn't see anything but a red light all around me. Then the red light began to waver and grow dim. I didn't feel any pain any more. A long time later, after you'd already found my body, suddenly I found myself among creatures who had been taken from the world by violence, just like my-

self. We all sat close together. We were cold. We were afraid
we might be forgotten. To be forgotten is the worst thing for
people like me in the other world, who can't go the same way
as the others who die peacefully.

"'But every time a friendly thought comes drifting over to
us, every time someone on earth remembers us kindly, then
the warmth of this loving thought streams over us and we
don't shiver so much.

"'It's a good thing that time doesn't mean anything with us.
Otherwise it would be an eternity for all of us. For until the
right time comes, who will find release? We must wait until
we can go with the one who murdered us before a court of
justice—where he can plead for mercy if we put in a good word
for him. Otherwise, he's lost and damned for all eternity.'

"You hear? That's the story little Margaret told me. Margaret
was my godchild. I loved her very much. When I heard she
was dead, I knew a man had murdered her. I didn't even have
to see her poor little ravished body."

The Covington, Kentucky, sheriff heard out the woman's
long story. She was completely convinced that the face in her
dream of the night before had been Margaret and that what
Margaret had said corresponded in all particulars with the
facts.

But it is not the way of the police to take dreams at face
value. They do not arrest someone for murder because a medium or a woman of mystical bent believes she has seen a face
in a dream.

However, this Ernest Foutch business could at least be
looked into. The heinousness of the crime made it a special
case. Horrible, without a clue left behind.

Margaret's body had been found buried in a field under a
few inches of dirt. Remarkably, she had sustained, besides her
neck wound, two shots through the head, entering behind the
ear.

They looked through the files for the name Ernest Foutch.
They discovered that earlier he had been involved in a sexual
offense against a young girl but, thanks to extenuating circumstances and a cleverly feigned mental disturbance, he had

been able to get off with a seven-year jail term. He now lived on the other side of Covington, in the opposite direction from where little Margaret's body had been found.

When it was decided to pay him a call, he was found lying in his room, drunk. But drunk or not, he was alert and diabolically quick-witted in his own defense during the questioning. Not until the sheriff began to recount the story that Margaret had told her aunt in her dream did Foutch turn pale.

"Who was there? Who heard me?"

"Foutch, that's all I need out of you. Someone only had a bad dream. But obviously the dream was true, down to the last detail. Or do you want to keep on denying it?"

Foutch shrugged. Little Margaret had cleared up the mystery of her own murder with a message from the other world.

Secrets of the beyond and of this world made known by third parties is the theme of the episodes being dealt with here. Communications of this kind, making use of a mediator, often come to public notice. From spiritualist séances and mediums' reports on dreams come alleged revelations of what it is like in another world. But here parapsychology keeps a cool head, which is needed to counter the hostility of the skeptics on the one hand and palpable liars and self-deceivers on the other.

It is one thing when doctors and psychologists impart information about the beyond gained verbatim at the bedside of some patient who died and was then brought back to life. It is quite another, and doubt immediately arises, when mediums claim to be able to clear the barrier between this world and the next at one swoop.

The father who demanded revenge for his daughter was a simple, rather primitive man who could not get the idea out of his head that he had lost his child under circumstances left unclarified by the police. Day and night he brooded about it. Finally he had all but figured out how the crime could have occurred. His imagination, always revolving about his daughter, generated a frightful dream picture of his daughter rising up in a menacing way to seek revenge through him.

A mysterious affair that took place during wartime forced its way to the surface from the subconscious of a person sensitized by a great preoccupation with occult matters, in such fashion that everything he said seemed to make sense.

The godmother, who had lived in Covington since earliest childhood, naturally knew about Ernest Foutch's past record. Foutch had already been found guilty of a sexual crime once when the godmother was young. She had forgotten about this —that is, forgotten it superficially. But her subconscious mind had carefully recorded this event from the past. And her subconscious now went to work and constructed a complete case: an accusation from a dead person, a finger pointing at the man who perpetrated the crime, a description of the circumstances of the case much more thorough than the police report. Strictly speaking, a woman with some imagination, hurt to the quick by the death of her godchild, could unconsciously have assembled this picture and experienced it in the form of a dream.

We cite these rational interpretations because in the scientific exploration of anything brought over into this world from the beyond, every last possibility of a natural explanation should be exhausted.

On the other hand, were occult factors actually involved in the foregoing incidents? Were intimations from the world beyond really projected into this world? So much the better for parapsychology if they were, so much the more interesting for research.

When one is seventy-five years old one cannot avoid thoughts about death from time to time. These thoughts leave me quite undisturbed, for I am firmly convinced that our spirit is an essence of completely indestructible nature; it is something that works on from eternity to eternity. It is like the sun, which seems to set only to our earthly eyes, but which really never sets, but shines on perpetually.

GOETHE, *Conversations with Eckermann*

8

"... And Then I Was Back on Earth Again."

IT HAD BEEN A BEAUTIFUL DAY. All day an azure blue sky had arched over the Scottish coast. Two days before, Michael Clifton had arrived at his brother Harry's house on the island of Islay to spend a long weekend.

Earlier the brothers had been talking a lot about their father, an eccentric millionaire and adventurer, John Talbot de Vere Clifton, who had traveled the world searching out secrets and mysteries. On these expeditions he had followed an old family saying, the motto on the Clifton coat-of-arms: "Triumph, or death."

Late in the afternoon, Michael Clifton, who four days before had celebrated his fortieth birthday, suddenly was seized by a cramp in his chest, so severe he could not breathe. Seconds later he collapsed. There was a good, capable country doctor on the island, and they fetched him to Michael's bed from a fishing trip on the coast. But all he was able to do was give Michael an injection to ease his pain. Meanwhile his condition worsened. Harry phoned Glasgow, and there got in touch with the chief of staff at the Western Infirmary.

"There's no point in my just coming over without equipment, Mr. Clifton. If we should find something that can't be taken care of on the spot, we might be losing a lot of valuable time. I can charter a plane here in Glasgow. The pilot knows the route to the island. We'll bring your brother back and save time."

An hour later a plane used on mercy flights to the Scottish islands landed on Islay. The chief of staff came along and examined the patient. The first injection had already lost its effectiveness. To ease Michael's torments, a second injection was given. Michael and his mother, Violet, were flown to the Western Infirmary.

In exactly an hour and fifty minutes Michael Clifton was lying on the operating table. They had to move fast. Special consideration had to be given to the heart. In all likelihood, complete anesthesia would bring complications.

Michael's seventy-four-year-old mother was keeping vigil outside in the waiting room, worrying about her son and feeling that she should be near him in these difficult hours.

Suddenly the operating-room door opened. Someone hurried out, quickly closing the door behind him. He seemed a little shaken. Mrs. Clifton inquired about the patient.

"We just lost him, Mrs. Clifton—on the operating table." Then he hastened away.

Yes—Michael Clifton was dead. His heart stood still. He no longer had a pulse. According to biological law, he was no longer a living person.

The chief of staff, who personally had taken charge of the operation, once more took careful stock of what had just happened. What in heaven's name could have caused Clifton's sudden demise? A thought flashed through his mind:

Clifton had had three injections, for analgesic purposes and in preparation for the operation. These three injections had worked against one another—collided, so to speak—with catastrophic effect. Now a man who, thanks to being operated on immediately, relieving him of his pain and saving him from the danger of internal hemorrhage from a perforated ulcer, was lying there dead.

Death ought not claim his prey so easily as that!

"Bring some ice! Get an icepack ready! Get him ready for going into the chest. The other operation has to be finished too. Don't lose any time!"

He knew that seconds could decide Clifton's permanent fate. Meanwhile, the chief of staff's assistants, the whole team, went to work like a single robot, quick and confident in every reach of their hands, every movement precise and cool. Now that the chief of staff had a glimmer of hope of saving the patient, during ensuing seconds and minutes the excessive loss of blood by the "dead man" had to be prevented. Michael Clifton lay dead for 120 seconds—for 2 full minutes dead as a stone. Then the surgeon's skilled hand took hold of the heart that had come to such a sudden stop. He massaged it, hoping by his manipulations to set it in motion again. He kneaded the heart muscle for 12 minutes, never stopping. His fingers hurt, grew numb. Then suddenly he felt the heart wall begin to react. It had stirred. Now it was working by itself. Its independent working would have to be supported gently.

A smile of triumph crossed the chief surgeon's face. He had brought it off! Michael Clifton was alive, had not died, as all had believed a short time before. Meanwhile, the operation on the stomach ulcer had been wrapped up as well.

The surgeon stayed at the patient's bedside for another three hours. Then Clifton opened his eyes. But he saw nothing— though the lids were open.

He screamed. But no one heard his voice.

He had come back from the afterworld, but he was blind, deaf, and paralyzed. Only his brain was awake. He was able to let it be known he was conscious by movements of his lips.

Blind, deaf, mute, and paralyzed! What a miserable prospect.

Violet Clifton sat weeping by his bed and tried to communicate with him by the pressure of her fingers. Was he aware that she was there? Was he as good as dead, a helpless vegetable who no longer saw the light of day, no longer heard the singing of the birds, was no longer able to talk with other people, no longer able even to lift himself from the bed where he lay?

Later he remembered what it had been like at this time.

"I lay in my eternal night and only in my brain knew I was still alive. I screamed into my brain: 'I won't die—I won't be a cripple—I won't lie here helpless.'

"And then I began to battle with myself. I observed my brain. I wanted to know whether death, which had seized me, had only partly let me go.

"I had experienced strange things. I had been on the other

side. I remember exactly how it was. The last thing I recall was the moment when I was wheeled into the operating room —and next thing, I was standing in front of a mountain all covered with flowers, all sorts of flowers. I saw a bright light in the distance, and this light approached me and filled me with a marvelous warmth.

"I heard sounds coming from this light, this warmth, music with a curious harmony. I saw people coming toward me. I wasn't able right off to make out who they were. But when I looked at them more closely I recognized them and spoke to them. They were all people who had died before me, friends killed in the war, a woman who had committed suicide out of love of a man.

"I saw these people and told myself that meeting them like this could only mean that I was dead too.

"This state of affairs, this sudden realization that it was all over for me, did not make me afraid. I simply waited for what would happen next.

"Presently something took me by the shoulder, by both shoulders. I was pulled back, back from the mountain with the flowers, back from the friends I had been talking to. I felt as if I were suddenly sliding down a steep slope. It became darker and darker around me. Just before this I had been in a state of wonderful bliss, but now I hurt unspeakably. Yes, I suffered horrible pain, a torment of pain in my chest, in my head. I felt someone touching my heart with his hand, holding on to my heart.

"And then I was back here on earth again. Night must have fallen. I heard nothing. I saw nothing. No one answered me. I couldn't move. But if someone touched me I felt it, a terrible agony. But—I couldn't cry out, I couldn't let anyone know I was suffering."

"Now a grim struggle began. Michael Clifton, the man who refused to die, who rebelled against being a helpless cripple, in the darkness of his night worked out a plan for finding his way back—to himself. He felt that his brain could think on only one track at a time. Therefore, he had to concentrate on one thing.

"I wanted to see, to perceive things around me. I thought for hours on end about seeing. I imagined all sorts of images in depth and color. I reviewed in my mind everything I had ever heard or read about the visual process. I knew that the eyes were not independent organs merely connected to the brain, but brain cells that had bulged out during an earlier stage of human development. If my brain was still functioning, if I could still imagine images, then I should also be able to see. They told me later it was fourteen days after I'd regained consciousness that I suddenly began to react to things moved before my eyes. I saw them as weak shadows."

They gave him red blankets, they hung a red cloth in the sickroom, to spur him on in his battle to live and see again.

Success encouraged him. He tried to learn how to speak. At first all that came from his lips was a senseless groaning and whispering. Then one day he did it. He was able to speak a real word. It was the first word he had learned as a child: "Mother—mother."

And then, in due course, some weeks later, he began to walk. At first it was all a staggering about and falling—as with a child. But now he was not going to give up. He knew that with iron will he could completely conquer death. His hearing had come back. He could hear sounds about him. He wanted to know from the doctor exactly how the brain worked, for he had become conscious of brain currents. He had discovered cerebral lead-paths perhaps never used before in his life. He felt that he had a double consciousness: a consciousness of his immediate environment and of the circumstances of his current existence; and a consciousness seated in the memory, now slowly surfacing in him.

The doctors came with small electrical devices and placed electrodes on his head. They stimulated this place and that, by sending currents through different points in the brain.

Clifton became conscious of music when they introduced a current at a point just above his ear. He heard a song and even believed he was singing it—yet the song was being sung only in his head, because an electrical stimulus had been applied and something in the brain cells responded.

They gave him no rest. His head was stimulated a square centimeter at a time. The doctors explained to him—the man who had been "in the hereafter"—that a too-protracted cooling of the brain cells had occurred during the minutes when he was for all intents and purposes dead. With that they had ceased to function, "once and for all."

But Michael Clifton's uncanny will, the will of a man who refused to stay dead, a will that grew out of the brain stem, hammered incessantly on these same cells like a strong electrical current coming from within. And with all the extreme concentration that Clifton was able to summon in his dark loneliness, his will zeroed in unconsciously on the brain cells, where the functions of thinking, feeling, and existing that had failed him have their seat.

Doctors and nurses all said the same thing.

"What he did was a miracle. We've never seen such a man. His will was so strong, he even forgot what it was to complain. Never a word, never a gesture of dissatisfaction, never a cross look. All he did was think and will—and will again. If you want the right word for it, it was a miracle of human willpower."

When Clifton's mother could no longer stand her helpless son's gibbering, she withdrew to a convent. What more could she do for him but pray? She stayed at the convent until she got a letter from him, in his newly learned, unfamiliar handwriting, in which he told her:

"I am alive again. I'm here again, Mummy. You know our family motto—triumph, or death. Well, I have triumphed over death. Certainly your prayers helped me. Or was it the doctors' skill?"

She went back to the hospital, and was overjoyed to see her son again.

"Has it occurred to you, perhaps, that your son is another person? After all, if a man was so far gone and came back, it could be that he . . ."

This question was put to Violet Clifton by Dr. J. P. McGown. She took her time answering him.

"Yes, he has become someone else. You're right. He's just

as nice and agreeable as before, Doctor. But there's still something different about him. He likes the nighttime now. Before, he was always happy when the sun came up and sorry when evening came; today, he loves the night passionately. He loves it as much as a man might love a woman or his country. I can feel it. I can feel how he is waiting for the world about him to grow softer when the light fails and sharp contours blur out.

"Often he will run out of the house in the middle of the night —I don't know where to. He walks through the streets. He must go off into the woods, too, for when he comes home his shoes are muddy and dirty."

Dr. McGown went on the lookout. He waited for eight nights. Then he solved the mystery. Nights Michael Clifton visited cemeteries. He sat on benches and seemed to enjoy his macabre surroundings. He would come back home calm, almost cheerful.

Dr. McGown never discussed his clandestine observations with Clifton. How, with a man who has already been in the beyond, to discuss his behavior on earth?

His father may have been a great adventurer, in the jungle, in the primeval forest, the desert, the Arctic—but Michael Clifton was the stronger, the braver. He accepted the challenge of the afterworld and measured up to it.

Thanks to sophisticated surgical techniques and quick emergency treatment, more and more people are being brought back from the dead. Michael Clifton is not an isolated case. Testifying to the return of a twenty-three-year-old nurse are the soberest of observer reports and a doctor who attended her during the critical phase.

The life story of the Bulgarian Penka Naidenova is a case in point. She came into the world in 1938 in a suburb of Sofia. When she was eighteen, she became a nurse, and worked in an operating room during the months just before the tragic event that was to change her life. Her job was to take care of surgical instruments and apparatus. While she was sterilizing some instruments, the incident occurred that was to make

Penka Naidenova a medical-world sensation. She became famous as the woman who demonstrably died, who was clinically dead for 120 minutes, and yet was awakened to a new
life.

On this day, she had washed the instruments and put them
in the sterilizer. In her left hand she had hold of an electric
cord carrying a current of 380 volts, and with her other hand
she reached out and turned on a water faucet. The current
from the cord shot through her arm, her chest, her whole body.
Then she fell to the floor.

A first determination of her condition came within seconds
from an assistant doctor kneeling beside her.

"Heartbeat no longer audible—can't feel any pulse." He immediately ordered artificial resuscitation. A cardiac specialist
was called. He at once made an injection into the cardiac region and a second directly into the heart. But after six minutes
there still were no heart sounds or pulse.

At this moment Dr. Pjotr Deredjan came through the station. He had known Penka Naidenova for years. Now it was a
matter of minutes.

"Let her lie where she is, don't move her. Put a tube into her
mouth, into the upper trachea—artificial breathing by intubation."

The doctors and nurses at the station took turns blowing air
into Penka Naidenova's lungs through the tube until the
anesthesia apparatus had been wheeled in to take over the job
automatically.

But Dr. Deredjan knew that intubation by itself would not
help. In a few terse words, he let the three operating-room
nurses know what he needed. And then he set about operating
on the dead woman as she lay before him on the floor. He
needed to go into the chest cavity lightning fast to expose the
pericardium, and massage the completely relaxed and immo-
bile heart without opening the pericardium.

"Somebody has to spell me right away. Massage as fast as
possible. The heart must be squeezed manually at least one
hundred twenty to one hundred forty times. Don't stop—don't
give up!"

Dr. Deredjan looked at his watch. Thirty minutes had passed. In thirty-seven minutes the heart began to flutter a little. "Get the electric-shock apparatus ready—give her a current of one hundred fifty volts for half a second."

After two shocks the fluttering stopped. The heart had gone still again. The massaging was resumed. In forty-three minutes the heart muscle began to contract normally, but as soon as the massage stopped, it stopped, too.

The people working on the dead woman were overcome by foreboding. They had already been at it for ninety minutes, all the while massaging the heart.

Then it happened. The wound made by opening the chest wall began to hemorrhage. The chest cavity filled with blood.

"We'll have to operate right now. Get everything ready in the operating room. We'll need twelve hundred fifty ccms of blood for transfusion. We know her blood group. Besides that, eight hundred eighty ccms of glucose solution. Light ether-oxygen anesthesia. Open a vein in her foot to take the glucose."

They continued to work for another 30 minutes. Then success. The heart was working—110 beats to the minute, blood pressure 120 over 60.

But the battle wasn't over yet. It continued for more than seventy-two hours. Penka Naidenova lay in a deep coma. Her chart read:

—Breathing normal.
—Blood pressure varying between 180 over 90 and 120 over 60.
—Pulse 150–160 per minute.

The doctors never took their eyes off their patient. Her circulation could break down any moment. The heart action had to be stabilized. At this point she did not react when spoken to. It was not until seventy-two hours later that she opened her eyes and turned her head in the direction of the voice that was trying to get her attention. She tried to say something, but was unable to do more than make sibilant sounds.

Slowly, life returned. Ten more days passed, and then the stricken woman began to speak: single words, brief sentences. She responded to questions and even knew her name. But she was unable yet to recognize anyone.

The electrocardiograms revealed severe damage to the heart muscle and other changes induced by oxygen deficiency. The heart sounds were muffled, their duration slightly extended. Beneath the rib cage they could feel a liver enlargement of four finger-widths.

Two months went by before Penka Naidenova could get up by herself and move about unassisted. She could use language again, but with a remarkable peculiarity: Although she could write perfectly, she could not read what she had written. Nor was she able to read a printed text. She would look at the single letters without being able to connect them and make sense out of them.

During this period her memory of what it had been like when she had been regarded as dead came back.

"I was in a strange world. The sun shone, and the meadows were green. I moved as easily as if I had wings. My grandmother sometimes used to tell me about paradise and heaven, and so now I saw heaven just as I had imagined it was as a child.

"I also met people, but now I can't remember just who they were. They seemed familiar to me, I'd seen them before. I keep trying to imagine what their faces were like so I can place them by name. But as time goes on everything gets less clear.

"One thing I can say for sure: In all my life I never knew such a feeling of happiness and contentment as I had in that wonderful, beautiful world. Did it last for minutes, hours? The idea of time had no meaning for me there."

Science has concluded from the Penka Naidenova case that the recuperative potential of the human cerebral cortex is much greater than in other creatures and that new lines of approach must be worked out for helping those who are at death's brink.

In any event, Penka Naidenova did become another personality. The changes in her psyche grew out of the events which
occurred that March 24th at 5:30 P.M. at Station 9 in the Sofia
hospital.

Think a great deal about death and think how, when you die, you are only shedding your hitherto sick body like so much old clothes in order to receive a more beautiful, a purer new body in the heavenly world in the company of creatures of bliss. Think a lot about this heavenly kingdom. This will give rise in you to an affinity with such heavenly kingdoms, so that nothing will do but that you come into one. If you fill your spirit with such thoughts, how can you still be sad, not to mention weep? More likely, quiet cheerfulness will take hold of you and you will be able to endure ailments calmly, come what may. What can happen, after all, except that you go to a heavenly world, if, as I have just said, you think so. And are you going to be afraid of that and weep about it? You should be overjoyed, and you can, if you follow my prescription. All people, all creatures whatsoever, have to die; even an illustrious person must. And people get upset by such thoughts. Do you get worked up when the sun goes down in the evening? Why not? Why should you, when tomorrow morning the sun will come up over the horizon again? We, too, sink down into death, only immediately to rise again in a new form. Actually, I have been thinking about death for years and from doing it have become ever more content within.

GEORG GRIMM

9

"I Spoke to My Darling in the Beyond!"

SINGER SERGE LAMA'S JOURNEY into the beyond began with a tragic auto accident.

On the road to Aix-en-Provence, his car went into a high-speed skid and slammed into a tree. Serge Lama felt his body being torn from the seat. He lost consciousness and did not come to until three days later, to find that in the interim the doctors had removed his spleen. He also learned that his heart had stopped during the operation, and with it clinical death had occurred. During this time he had had a strange and gripping experience.

At first he became aware of a great explosion of light. The garishly white, blinding light was like a magnesium flare. The thunderous crashing sound of his collision was still reverberating in his ears when he felt himself suddenly being possessed of an enormous strength. Another self seemed slowly to detach itself from his body. The phenomenon was like the duplication of dying persons often observed by mediums. According to his own story, the singer's spiritual body hovered above his completely shattered physical one. All pain vanished at the moment the insubstantial body began to detach itself.

At the same time, he became aware of a sobbing sound nearby. With some difficulty he succeeded in opening his eyes. He saw, in ghostly silhouette, the woman, his lover, who had been seated beside him in the car. However, when Lama started to follow her, the girl retreated from him. He was prevented from catching up with her by an invisible barrier he could not cross. He remained behind this mysterious barrier while his mistress's form completely disappeared.

Instead, looking around, Lama now saw wonderful images

of places he felt sure he had been before, images corroborating his assumption that he must have lived on earth more than once. For example, there appeared to him an inn located in Carcassonne, an old town in the south of France whose fortified walls were built under Visigoth rule in the fifth century. Lama had been there with a group of artists during a musical tour. At that time, the minute he had stepped into the inn where he was to stay, he had felt certain that he had been there before, a very long time before. He remembered the three steps, the thick walls, the ceiling beams, the wooden staircase going upstairs.

All that had been some years before. But now, in his state of detachment from his physical body, suddenly an image of the same medieval inn materialized out there in the beyond. The singer saw himself inside the inn wearing a monk's brown cowl and surrounded by other men. Obviously, they were all in hiding. Suddenly armed men burst into the room. He heard cursing; there was a struggle. When the soldiers began to get the upper hand, Lama saw himself in the cellar and from there fleeing through a trapdoor into a passageway leading to freedom.

Outside the sky was lit up red, and he knew at once what that signified: the fires of the auto-da-fé had been kindled. Lama knew immediately when he watched these happenings why this blurred picture of a vaulted cellar from an earlier life had remained in his memory.

About the year 1209, during the Albigensian wars, the Cathari were savagely suppressed in Carcassonne. The Cathari sect, from the end of the tenth to the middle of the fifteenth century, spread throughout southern and western Europe under a variety of names. The Cathari (the word comes from the Greek and means "the pure," and from it also comes the German word for heretic, *Ketzer*) aimed at restoring Jesus' pure teachings. At that time Serge Lama was one of the Catharist monks who barely escaped with their lives from Crusade troops under Simon de Montfort and so from the Inquisition and death at the stake.

To blot out this terrible vision for a time, the singer held his hands over his eyes. When he took them away, another picture was there in perfect clarity.

Before his eyes sprang into shape the inner courtyard of a town house in the old Quartier de Marais in Paris. Serge Lama saw himself standing there embracing a young woman wearing a long crinoline dress, a girl who bore a curious resemblance to his recently vanished mistress. In the distance he heard the angry tumult made by masses of people gathered at the Bastille. It was a parting kiss that he was watching in the courtyard. The young woman must have been an aristocrat whose life was in peril, for she whispered: "If they arrest me, I'll scratch a little cross here on this stone. If you find it, you'll know they've taken me to the scaffold." She pointed at a wall near the window ledge.

His return to life was accompanied by a resumption of intense pain in his broken bones and torn muscles. The waves of pain flooded into his brain. When Lama opened his eyes, he found himself in casts in a hospital bed. A doctor was saying something to him, but he was still in no condition to grasp the sense of it. Only one thing encouraged him: a clear realization that once again he had overcome death.

After Lama had completely gained consciousness, he learned that his mistress and a friend, Enrico Macias, who had also been in the car, had died of their injuries.

The singer was bedridden and unable to walk for two years. When he was finally able to get about again, with the help of crutches, the first thing he did was go by taxi to the Quartier de Marais. At the town house he had seen in the afterworld, he found the right window ledge. The little cross he was seeking was scratched on a dirty gray cornerstone.

For sixteen years Charles Aznavour, the famous French popular singer, kept silent. Then he decided to talk about the experiences he had gone through after his auto accident on August 31, 1956, near Brignoles. The description of what this artist heard and saw during his hours of clinical death goes, in his own words, as follows:

"Too late to avoid him—the truck had popped up so suddenly that when the collision came all I could do was hang on desperately to the steering wheel. I heard a crash and my nose and forehead smashed into the windshield and a sharp object bored through my thigh. Then I lost consciousness, until I got the idea that there hadn't been an accident at all, that my car had merely come to a stop.

"I tried to lift my right arm to my face, but the arm wouldn't work. However, this didn't bother me, for I was now in a quiet world filled with a vivid rose-colored mist. At the same time, I was still sitting on the driver's seat of my car. In all events, I had lost all sense of time and was no longer able to tell whether the car had been stopped for minutes or hours. I was filled with a powerful feeling of well-being, heightened by a comfortable warmth that was seeping through my body.

"Suddenly I heard a voice say: 'My God, he's dead!'

"These words led me to ask myself whom they could be talking about, and I began to be concerned about my two passengers, Claude Figus and Leccia. Meanwhile, I was being lifted out of the wreck. The reddish mist was still all around me, and I couldn't make out who the people were. All that I heard was: 'Help the others first. This one is dead.'

"Obviously they meant me.

"They laid me down, stretched out, on the ground. I tried to tell the people helping us that nothing serious was the matter with me, but I got the impression I was not being heard. Anyway, I heard myself shout loudly: 'Help him! Help him!' By him I meant Claude Figus.

"Then I felt my clothing being opened and someone pressing his head on my chest.

"'You're right, he's dead. His heart's not beating any more.'

"This time the voice sounded very close to my ear.

"It now became clear they were indeed talking about me. Somehow a great feeling of relief came over me. So this was what it was like to be dead, the one thing we'd always been afraid of, the thing looked on as a frightful bogey—this complete stillness, this inner peace, this delicately reddish mist! I asked myself why I had ever been afraid of it at all, for obviously there wasn't the slightest reason.

"But suddenly I was gripped with horror, making me cry out loudly in terror. I put every ounce of strength I had left into it, for all at once I knew I wasn't really dead after all. For wasn't I aware of sounds from the world of the living; couldn't I hear the voices of the police, hissy whisperings, the squealing of brakes, the loud hails of inquisitive drivers stopping at the scene of the accident? Faced with these facts, it seemed absolutely necessary for me to make myself noticed, to let the people around me know I was still alive so they could help me.

"I screamed and screamed loudly, but nobody seemed to pay any attention, although I could plainly make out shadowy figures moving through the reddish mist. But suddenly I saw no more. All I could feel was something touching my eyes, and then a big black curtain sank down in front of me. It seemed to me that a policeman must have closed my eyes and spread a blanket over my body.

"After this happened, I was only a corpse at the edge of the road to the people assisting at the accident, requiring no further attention at the moment. However, I kept up my screaming and yelling, until presently I noticed I was being moved to some other place. I drew on my last reserves of willpower to grasp what was happening to me, for I had become aware of new sounds and at first I couldn't tell where they were coming from.

"Then, like lightning, the thought came to me that I wasn't at the accident site on the highway under a woolen blanket any more, but in my own coffin.

"A soft sobbing filled me with gratification: My first wife, Evelyn, had come to my burial service! She was standing beside the big silver-mounted sarcophagus in the little Russian church I knew so well. The church was filled with people. Again I was shaken by feelings of dread, and the rosy mist made me very restless. I wanted to cry out and let everyone there know that I was still alive. Bury me? That just couldn't happen! Although I was lying inside my own coffin, I could still see the outside of the sarcophagus. In short, I was consciously taking part in my own burial.

"Some people came up to me with censers of incense. Incense was the favorite scent of my childhood, and I breathed in the fumes with deep pleasure. I'll never in my life forget the sensation of the pleasant smell. The mourners slowly left the church. I was carried out, which dispersed the strong incense odor and replaced it with a stale, depressing smell of rot. I now became aware that my body was decomposing. I asked myself when all this had happened, in what decade, what century, but could find no answer. In my coffin, carried out by people unknown to me, I shrieked and raved. I didn't want to decay in this narrowness, for I was very much alive. But the others believed I was dead. The smell of putrefaction, growing ever more penetrating, made it clear to me that my fate was sealed irrevocably.

"Then a voice pierced the stillness: 'Calm yourself, please, Monsieur Aznavour.'

"My tightly shut eyes opened, and I saw that a nurse was bending over my bed and cleaning my face with a swab of cotton. That held the odor that had been horrifying me. Now again I felt severe pains, growing ever more unbearable. My upper parts were tied down to the bed."

Charles Aznavour whispered: "I feel very bad." At this point the nurse confirmed what had been going on through his head.

"You were far gone, way off, when we revived you. They'd already written you off as dead. Your heart stopped, and you didn't begin to breathe again until it had been massaged."

During his long career, American psychologist Dr. Ben Roberts has given intensive study to the dying process. He confirms the experience of many doctors, namely, that the dying are almost always willing to pass on, and that it is not death itself but the business of dying that people fear. He asserts, of people at death's threshold:

"They seem to know something that we who are healthy and not looking death in the eye cannot understand. One might almost believe that the patient, in the last few minutes of his life, in full consciousness finds himself in two worlds:

in the one we are familiar with and in another that we call life after death.

"Many doctors who have stayed with their patients until the last moment will doubtless remember how a dying person will suddenly greet a deceased relative, or memorably describe a scene in nature, a garden, or a walk. It's as if some sort of passageway had suddenly opened up in front of the dying person, allowing him to describe what he is seeing as he passes through it."

Dr. Roberts is well acquainted with the case of ten-year-old Hans Borgmann, who was crushed under a wall when it collapsed.

Hans lay in the hospital for days in a deep coma. Dr. Paul Klein, who took care of him, stated that "twice during those five days the boy was clinically dead."

What Hans Borgmann related to Dr. Klein after he recovered is a proof of another life beyond the grave:

"I felt wonderful. So wonderful, I only hoped never to lose the feeling. Twice I visited another country. There were a lot of children there playing outdoors and in big, golden cities. I wanted to play with them, but they told me I wouldn't have time.

"The first time I went away I saw children outdoors, with such wonderful toys, I didn't want ever to go away. They had instruments which they made nice music with and flowers that you could see growing. The second time I saw a great big city made of solid gold and filled with kids. They were so happy. We laughed together. When everything disappeared all of a sudden, I was awfully sad, because I knew I had to come back here."

Dr. Roberts's view is also held by his colleague Dr. Isaac Simons of Toronto, Canada:

"Man has learned a little about how our physical body functions, but up to the present he has been unable to fathom the real basis of life. Call it what you will—supernatural power, a form of energy, vibrations, or soul—everyone must admit that a human being consists of more than flesh, bones, and muscle.

It is perfectly conceivable that what we call life can exist before our earthly body is born and continue to exist after the body's death."

Among other things, he cites his own experiences with a patient who died as the result of an auto accident.

Mrs. Sandra Farrell was a thirty-year-old housewife with two children. She set out with her husband to visit friends; on the way the car collided with a big truck.

Mrs. Farrell was brought to the hospital unconscious.

"She had lost a great deal of blood and sustained a number of grave internal injuries," Dr. Simons reports. "Late at night her heart stopped beating, and a team of specialists had to work on her for five or six minutes to bring her back to life."

Dr. Simons feared the worst if she were told about her husband's death. Going down the long corridor to her room, he debated whether the tragic news should be kept from her for a while. He opened the door, but before he could utter a word his patient looked into his eyes and whispered:

"It's all right, Dr. Simons. I know my husband is dead."

She must have seen the thunderstruck expression on the doctor's face. For right then and there she launched into an explanation. She knew what had happened to her husband, she said, because she had seen him herself when she was clinically dead:

"I know I died, because I could feel how my heart had stopped beating. I remember thinking: 'This is the end!' Then I floated farther and farther away. Suddenly I found myself on a meadow path, but had the feeling, when I walked, that my feet weren't touching the ground. But I wasn't the least bit surprised to be over there. Nor was I surprised when I ran into my husband, John.

"I wanted terribly to keep on going beside John. It was so peaceful and fine, and I felt ever so happy. But John wouldn't have it. He very gently turned me around and said I'd have to go back for a time.

"Don't think I'm sad because he's gone from me. I know he's happy, and besides that, I'm sure I'll see him again."

Men are not disquieted by things themselves, but by their ideas of things. For example, death is not frightful, or else it would have had to appear frightful even to a Socrates. No, the idea that death is frightful is the frightful thing.

EPICTETUS (A.D. c. 50–c. 138)

10

Counterfeit Death?

"At last I was perfectly calm. I knew now for sure nothing could be changed. Near me someone had gone wild in a last sudden flareup of the will to live, thrashing about with arms and legs and . . .

"It had done no good. He was bound to a post just like myself.

"And then they shot at me. I had closed my eyes and knew it would be all over in a flash.

"Then I felt a blow on my chest. I didn't even hear the shot —or shots. Perhaps the bullet came faster than the sound. In any case, I was hit only once, and was amazed that I felt no pain.

"My eyes had been bandaged, and besides that, I had closed my eyelids. Naturally, everything was dark.

"I felt myself going all weak inside. No doubt I collapsed.

"But I wasn't afraid, nor did I feel any pain. All that I felt was the darkness soothing me and the sensation of going weak that was like a deliverance.

"And then I felt another blow, on my head—exactly like the one before on my chest. I started to tell myself it must have been the *coup de grâce*. But now that I think back on it, to tell the truth, I never really finished this thought.

"It was all over. Absolutely finished.

"What else did I feel? Now, that's really something. After it was all over, after the blow on my head, after quite a while of just nothingness, I suddenly felt that I was in an elevator, or in any case sitting in a narrow tube, and rushing downward at tremendous speed. And yet not always downward. Suddenly I slid to one side—just as fast sideways as down, first to the left, then to the right—then up this time. Yet finally I was shooting downward again.

"During this elevator ride I got astonishingly hot. I still remember that the warmth was pleasing to me. But why I felt that way and what I was thinking, naturally I don't recall.

"In any event, suddenly I saw a figure in front of me. It was neither man nor woman but had a white face. I called out to it, this figure, saying it should show me the way. But it made no reply because—I've just remembered it now—because it had no mouth. It took me by the hand and led me over a bridge. Dark blue water was running under this bridge. I wanted more than anything to stop and look down into the water. But the figure dragged me along. Or more like constrained me to keep pace. I was quite lost here and had to follow along.

"Suddenly, in the middle of the bridge, the phantom stopped, looked at me, let go of my hand, and went off rapidly in the opposite direction. Now I was standing alone on the bridge and unable to move ahead, because all of a sudden the span ahead of me was completely broken and led nowhere at all. I ran back, as fast as I could. I speeded up even more because the bridge was crumbling behind me . . .

"What day is it today?"

"January seventeenth."

"January seventeenth? My execution was supposed to have taken place on November nineteenth. Where have I been all this time?"

"Don't think about that yet. It'll all come back to you anyway. Perhaps you've been on that bridge you were telling about."

"How is it possible I'm still living?"

"An exception, a miracle. There are such cases, you know. We got you out of the burial pit in the nick of time . . . something about your body made us notice you. Then we sewed up your heart, and after a while, when we'd got some life into you, we tried a brain operation, very, very carefully. You simply were lucky."

"A man shot through the heart and head can still live?"

"Otherwise you wouldn't be here."

"Maybe I was already dead. Perhaps that shaft, that tube I was traveling through, and then that figure leading me over the bridge . . ."

The man who had been executed only to live—or to live again—said no more. It all seemed so incomprehensible to him that he should still be there. The doctor at his bedside changed the subject. It would not do for the patient, just saved from the grave, to lose himself too much in his thoughts. The doctor preferred to talk about the techniques making it possible to restore to life someone who should have been long dead.

"It's possible that a man with a pierced heart can still hang on for quite a while and in a way expire gradually. Some classic cases in medicine demonstrate that death may not ensue for some hours even after the heart has been completely penetrated. If a person with a wound of this sort can be gotten to the hospital without removing the penetrating object, the victim's chances of being saved are even greater, since the blood being lost from the wound will only seep out instead of emptying in a gush. Sewing up a heart wound is a perfectly routine operation, and needlelike penetrations of the heart are not especially dangerous at all.

"However, bullet wounds are basically difficult, because the heart is highly susceptible to heavy impacts. Still, a year or more ago I personally was able to save the life of a policeman whose right ventricle had been shot through near the tip. And you are the second case."

"But my brain! After all, a shot through the head . . ."

"Some years ago a suicide was brought in to us. He had put five revolver shots into the upper right temporal region. Another man shot himself twice in the head at eyebrow level between the eye and the ear. The brain pan was smashed open. Brain tissue even came out. But both these men were saved.

"But it's a double miracle in your case, because you've survived both a shot through the heart and one through the head —a *coup de grâce*, as they call it."

"You mean to tell me that I didn't really die after all that? I still keep thinking about that bridge and that phantom and

the shaft I was sliding through where it was so narrow and I
got so hot . . ."

The doctor shrugged.

"We try to save people whenever there's a spark of life left
in them. But whether it's possible to bring back someone who's
already dead—well, who can say that with certainty?"

John Forth, a master machinist at a large New York generat-
ing plant, gave the following description to the doctors who
had brought him back to life after electrocution.

He had been quite sure there could be no current running
through this high-voltage cable. He reached for the wire
and . . .

"It was as if my brain had been struck by a bolt of lightning.
Then I had the feeling that the inside of my head was stuffed
with wadding, black wadding. Suddenly I was stuck in black
wadding and could see that my head—that's right, my head—
was filled with nothing but light. And this light gave off a
hissing sound. I tried to free myself from the black wadding.

"Then, suddenly, the hissing stopped and the light went out.
Way off in the distance I heard someone coughing and then a
person laughing. Was it really a laugh, though?

"I'm not sure about it now. It could have been the echo of
something falling to the ground. But there was no ground there,
nothing but black wadding everywhere.

"Now I remember something else. Just came to me. When
this pang went through my brain, when I felt the lightning in
my head, I said to myself, 'I'm not willing to die!'

"For the moment the lightning flashed, I knew I'd touched
a live wire. It came all at once, the feeling of lightning, the
feeling of having my head filled with black wadding and the
thought I'd touched a wire that would kill me. Yet at the same
moment I set my mind against it and told myself, 'I will not
die.'

"But then, as I waded through the black wadding, I stopped
thinking altogether. After a while I found that even the
wadding had stopped being uncomfortable. It was really
beautifully soft. Supposing I were to lie down in it and go to
sleep?

"But as I started to lie down, I saw I was absolutely wrong. I had only dreamed up the black wadding. I had just imagined everything. And where everything had just been black was now a deep orange.

"More than that I don't remember.

"But if I'm back here now and alive—then I suppose you must have tried all sorts of things on me to bring me to. Right?"

Naturally, every possible resuscitative means had been used. For twelve straight hours every known revival technique had been applied. The body had been wrapped in blankets and towels, hot-water bottles and heating pads applied, in an attempt to compensate for the heat loss that had set in. In the doctors' opinion, had the cooling of the body progressed further, clinical death would have been a certainty. Then, after a lapse of twelve hours, a specialist from the famous Johns Hopkins Medical School arrived and tried his new system of counter-shock. He attached an electrode to the chest and another to the back and sent a low amperage current through the heart.

Immediately John Forth began to stir. What previous resuscitation methods had been unable to accomplish was achieved by the counter-shock technique, a method that the doctor had tried out on thousands of animals before using it on human beings.

"And what do you make of Forth's description of his experience? I mean, this business about the black wadding and the rest. Do you suppose it all could have been actual phenomena arising out of contact with another world?"

"Well, he was very close to the edge. But had he crossed over to the other side? I really can't say about that. I've saved a dozen people who were in the same state as Forth. Most of them didn't talk about how it had been with them. They didn't want to listen to questions and seemed almost angry when they were pressed to say what it was like while they were knocked out, or how it felt when the crucial shock hit the body.

"And then again, with others we've had a variety of statements. For example, an electrical engineer told me he had the sensation of sliding down a very thin, brilliantly incandescent brass rod. What Forth experienced as a lightning flash with the engineer was perhaps the brass rod.

"Another one—a very simple man—gave me quite another kind of report. He took a fall on a mountainside, was sent hurtling by a rocky projection out into space, and struck a high-tension wire on the way down. In this case, by the way, the man died later of his burns.

"He said he encountered a host of bright figures. He had been picked up, he said, and taken into a circle of these figures, after which he felt very well. He also claimed to have recognized two of the figures, one a friend of his youth, the other his own father. He assured me that these figures had moved about in a spherical sort of space which seemed to be steeped in a lilac color.

"But naturally, we doctors and psychiatrists have to be very skeptical. As long as the brain is working, as long as the brain cells are not destroyed and able to function, naturally stimuli can arise in the central nervous system and create illusions not subject to normal criteria, since the stimuli themselves are not normal. Somehow the victim's wishes and hopes and very early ideational orientations can decisively influence the images that then appear.

"But who knows exactly? We're all groping . . ."

"Have you ever had a chance, for experimental purposes, to get hold of a man who had been executed in the electric chair? If a person like that could ever be brought back to life, he must have experienced very strange images indeed."

"Now you're talking like one of us. You may know that sometimes the very highest voltages do not necessarily kill, whereas in one case twenty-seven volts was enough to do the job. On the other hand, as I say, I have seen someone who took fifty-five thousand volts and lived through it.

"A readiness to die, or the fear of dying, or the conviction that death is unavoidable, all play an important role. Consider people when they are asleep. Then even the heaviest electric shocks are relatively not dangerous—even when they are powerful enough to cause deep burns. The critical thing is the paralysis of the breathing center in the brain. If this happens, death follows by the accumulation of poisons in the circulatory system. Short of incinerating them, we have been unable to kill turtles and frogs with electric current.

"But a person who is put into an electric chair and then has a copper headpiece attached to his head, right down on the parietal area, is convinced then and there that his end has come. He is now resigned to die, a state that grows more ominous every second. Then, beyond this, there is the heat effect of the current, which flows directly from the copper headplate into the gray matter of the brain and which can be destroyed by excessive heat.

"Naturally, exceptions can occur, and it's quite true that men in the electric chair have only been knocked unconscious and died later on the dissecting table.

"In most cases of accidents with high-voltage wires the victim touches the wire with an arm or a foot and the current then leaves the body by the shortest and quickest route. If John Forth had touched the live wire with his left hand in such a way that the current emerged from his right leg, then probably we'd never have been able to revive him. Forth was a lucky man."

"And his trip through the black wadding?"

"I don't know what to say about that. He may well have been very close to the brink. Perhaps some day we'll know more about it."

The main thing for the Johns Hopkins doctor was having saved many lives. Lacking hard evidence, he had no interest in speculation on the afterworld. But the conjectures of well-known thinkers are founded on a profusion of material. The philosopher C. J. Ducasse cites several possibilities.

Either the psyche lives on in a condition like that of the unconsciousness of the dying and thus can retain a loose relationship with the living world by faintly remembering names, events, and ideas, or psychic existence simply runs its course, as in the experience of dreams. It is also not out of the question that a continued life of the psyche may be linked with creative thought. If, for instance, we think in this connection of music or philosophy, we must take into account here that we have only earthly notions, which on higher levels of intelligence could become different concepts.

It may also be possible to gain meaning for life after death by the evaluation of mundane experiences, whereby new perspectives might arise on forms of awareness at present beyond the earth-dweller's grasp.

The possibility of different developmental levels is also worthy of consideration, likewise that beings of the beyond may be able to communicate by telepathy with other psyches, even those mantled in mortal flesh.

❦

And when Lachesis has no more thread, it frees itself from the flesh, and
  bears away in potency both the human and divine;
the other powers, the whole of them mute;
    memory, intelligence and will, keener far in action than they were
    before
Staying not, it falls of itself in wondrous wise to one of the shores; there
  it first learns its way.
Soon as it is circumscribed in place there, the formative virtue radiates
  around in form and quantity as the living members;
and the air, where it is full saturate, becomes decked with divers colors
  through another's rays which are reflected in it,
so the neighboring air sets itself into that form which the soul that is
  there fixed impresses upon it by means of its virtue;
and then, like the flame which follows the fire wheresoever it moves,
  the spirit is followed by its new form.
Inasmuch as therefrom it afterwards has its semblance, it is called a
  shade; and therefrom it forms the organs of every sense even to sight.
By this we speak, and by this we laugh, by this we make the tears and
  the sighs which thou mayst have heard about the mount.
The shade takes its form according as the desires and the other affec-
  tions prick us, and this is the cause of whereof thou marvellest.

DANTE ALIGHIERI (1265–1321),
The Divine Comedy, "Purgatory," Canto XXV

11

The Suicide
of Red Square

As DAY DAWNED over Red Square, one of the soldiers on guard at Lenin's Tomb caught sight of a strange shadowy figure at the iron grill work of a large building across the way. When it came time for the watch to change, the guardsman reported what he had seen. It turned out that a man had hanged himself from the bars on account of some foolish thing that with an ordinary person would have never justified such a drastic move: A woman had abandoned him.

But the romance is another story, of no relevance here.

On this very same early morning, not far from Red Square Professor Brunchanenko was still at work with his seven assistants. They had been at it all night, carrying out artificial-heart experiments on animals. A few days before, these experiments had yielded very positive results. They had succeeded in bringing a dog back to life for six hours, genuinely alive and with all vital reactions.

One of the officers of the guard had heard of these experiments. He also knew that the work was going on right at that moment. And so he phoned Professor Brunchanenko and inquired whether he would like to have the suicide's body sent over.

For a moment Brunchanenko hesitated. Then an idea came to mind.

"Yes, send him over—but fast, and don't move him about too much. Lay him down perfectly flat. And don't do anything to him. Hurry up, now."

Thus the hanged man of Red Square came into Professor

Brunchanenko's laboratories. The artificial-heart machine was attached to a man unquestionably dead. The machine began to pump, pulsing blood into arteries that seemed already lax and defunct. Again and again spurts of blood were forced into the dead man's system, blood to which oxygen and some cardiac stimulants had been carefully added.

The pumping in and sucking out of the blood proceeded with absolute precision. Electrical controls regulated the pulse of the artificial heart with perfect accuracy. Great patience was in order—hours of waiting. But at last the goal toward which they were striving was reached. The artificial-heart machine brought the hanged man of Red Square back to a new existence. To be sure, this life renewed was a weak thing, hanging by a thread. After all, in hanging himself he had severely damaged his larynx and jammed his tongue down his throat. Moreover, many changes had taken place throughout his whole body, deteriorations that are signs of death for those at all skilled in such matters.

For instance, the muscles had completely lost their ability to contract. They showed no reaction when stimuli were applied with electrodes. This indicated that the man must have been swinging a long time from the grating. The dilation of the pupils that occurs when the death agony is finished had long since come and gone. The pupils had contracted to less than their usual diameter. The eyeballs themselves had become soft and shrunken.

The skin had a parchment feel. When hot sealing wax was dropped onto it to see if it would cause a blister, the effect was negligible. The livid spots typical of a corpse had yet to appear. But the body was very cold.

"No question about it, his temperature will have to be raised. When organic oxidation stops, naturally the body heat drops. It was very cold outdoors this morning, too. The body has a lower temperature reading than the thermometer outside."

All available means were now brought to bear: slowly heated oil baths, electric heating pads wrapped about the limbs. Meanwhile, the artificial heart pulsed on, sending richly oxygenated blood into the arteries.

"He just moved his lips! He wants to say something, or—"

At this moment they heard a long, groaning sigh issue from the mouth of the man who had hanged himself in Red Square.

"We've got this far, anyway. Now we've got to keep cool and keep going—just as long as the machines keep functioning. We've got to make it!"

The artificial-heart machine pumped on and on, pouring life into a dead man from whom the only response so far had been a single sigh.

The next day the resuscitative process had reached a point at which the man was able to speak in whispers. The brain had begun to function again.

"I was in a country where I'd never been before.

"It was very big there, and so beautiful. I'd like to go back there again.

"I can still taste the sweet water that I drank there. For there was a fountain there and I drank out of it.

"I saw flowers that were three times as big as ours. They smelled sweeter than the prettiest flowers we have here at the height of summer.

"I saw a lot of people a great distance away. When I started to run toward them, they moved away from me just as fast.

"There was a drummer standing under a giant tree that seemed to reach the sky. This drummer didn't run away from me. He just stood there beating on his drum until I was close to him.

"I don't know whether it was he, but someone spoke to me. Someone said to me that everything was all right now and that I could fly, too, if I wanted.

"How heavy my arms and legs are now. I don't think I'll ever be able to move them again, for in that other land where I was, everything was light as a feather. If only those people hadn't kept running away from me.

"The drummer grew as big as the tree. I couldn't see his face any more. And then I started to run through all the beautiful greenness and to call out loud for someone. Now I know it was my mother I was looking for. But she has been dead a long time. Anyway, I went looking for her and someone told me

I'd find her soon. But it'll still take quite a while. It's always a long time before you find the one you're looking for.

"Then I fell asleep under the big tree that reached way up into the sky.

"Now I'm not sure whether life in that other land was just a dream. Or whether I'm having a bad dream now."

They put many questions to this man who had crossed death's threshold. He lived on for four days. Then suddenly even the artificial heart seemed no longer able to hold him in the land of the living.

"I long to get back to the green land!" he whispered before he died. These were the last words to come from the mouth of the man who hanged himself in Red Square.

A good deal has been written in scientific literature about "the suicide of Red Square." He is cited as an interesting case of the revival of a person apparently dead, with the stipulation that in hangings death is apparently delayed for some time unless there has been a drop of at least 2 meters, or about 6.5 feet, to ensure enough impact to break the cervical vertebrae. But the case is also described as a classic example of resuscitating, albeit briefly, a dead human being. After all, similar experiments had been done for years on animals in an attempt to gain information on the extent to which it is possible, by the use of blood and oxygen, to restore some degree of functioning to dead warm-blooded animals.

Naturally, the reports filed at the institute by Professor Brunchanenko had to be highly conservative, not because they were written in Moscow, but because only those functions accessible to strict biological control could be tested.

The cord, as it tightened, had exerted pressure on the cervical vertebrae at a point where certain nerve branches come out of the spinal cord. At issue were these ganglia, through which, as is known from other hanging cases, a curious state of excitation is induced in the last seconds of the terminal agony.

To this day only one man in the world is known who could not be hanged. He was a yogi who was able to train his throat, his nerves, and his neck muscles to resist the critical pressure, a pressure at once paralyzing and excitatory. Not even his wind could be throttled off.

According to the Moscow report on the suicide of Red Square, the anomalies in the man's brain logically to be expected after a cutoff of the cerebral blood supply did in fact occur. After all, his air had been cut off, and the supply of oxygenated blood interrupted. As a result, stimuli of a physical and psychological nature occurred that affected the senses of color and hearing. And now came this perfectly clear and sober conclusion:

The scenes described by the man restored to new life with the aid of the artificial-heart machine can be explained only on purely biological grounds.

In the opinion of all psychobiologists, man is a biological creature equipped with an organization of reflex systems. These reflex systems, made up of nerve tracts, have a leading role in the life of the organism. They run from the surface of the body via the spinal cord into the cortex of the brain, where other neurons have the task of tying the nerve tracts together. Thence efferent nerves run from the brain to the expressive organs—for example, to the muscles, cell tissue, and glands.

Each nervous system, consisting of afferent and efferent nerve tracts, has a certain function. These functions are the reflexes. In a sense, a nerve is a tube or wire through which neural current flows. There is a close parallel with the system of vessels through which the blood flows.

In the cortex, or rind, of the brain are found nerve cells that have been given the name of thought cells. These thought cells are the organs of consciousness. In the view of psychobiology, consciousness is no more than the high point of the functioning of the nuclei in the thought cells. From this activity comes a feeling that is called consciousness. Viewed in this fashion, the loss or restoration of consciousness is a purely physical event, needing no metaphysical or metapsychic explanation.

Psychobiology goes even further. In the cortex a distinction is made between the small pyramidal cells (sympathetic nervous system), the large pyramidal cells (sensory nervous system), and finally those layered cells that have no direct peripheral connection, but that to a degree function "vegeta-tively," energized by impulses from the sympathetic and sen-sory cells of the cortex.

The sensation of consciousness is ascribed to the small pyra-midal cells. The large pyramidal cells are considered to be involved in the apprehension of objects, while the conceptual and memory cells are found in layers of what are called poly-morphous cells, cells that, as already noted, have no direct con-nection with conscious existence.

In other words, consciousness is merely a property of the functioning of the thought cells. Psychobiology conceives this functioning to be an absolutely unalloyed biological event.

But how about the unconscious? And dreams?

The reflex systems, we are told, and especially in the thought cells, have various grades or levels of activity, governed by concepts as they occur, and by the memory cells as they be-come operative. In sum, the subconscious and the unconscious are nothing more than functional levels!

If, then, all psychophysical events are functions of the neural system, from the standpoint of psychobiology there can be only one interpretation of the experience described by the suicide of Red Square:

Because of the interruption of the blood supply and the con-sequent cutting off of nourishment for the brain cells, drastic anomalies arose in the functioning of the cortex and its thought cells, including those identified with memory. Everything that the suicide saw or felt when the temporarily benumbed and al-most defunct cells were again beginning to respond repre-sented cortical malfunction, as distinguished from normal function. These malfunctionings arose because things the hanged man perhaps had been told in his youth, descriptions of other countries, themes from fairy tales and legend or re-ligious imagery, had taken hold in the polymorphous cells and surfaced when, as it were, the layers of gray matter began to work again from the bottom up.

Malfunctionings? Nothing more than malfunctionings?

How can such delicate structures as thought cells function normally and soundly when changes in their nourishment produce conditions they cannot cope with over the long run and which must surely kill them?

In this connection, psychobiology goes so far as to contend that all neuroses can be explained on a purely biological basis. In the cortex, where the cells of consciousness are located, a functional disturbance has taken place, as a result of which the neurotic is caught up in a world either primitively oriented, or subject to eruptions of primitivity so strong that they override the higher developmental levels of consciousness.

The suicide of Red Square was a simple fellow. His cortex, his organ of consciousness and memory, had been trained very little in rigors of an intellectual nature. That is, his cortical cells had had little functional exercise. Thus, when his cortex dried out, so to speak, and the nourishment of the cells was then resumed, the result was a mixture of subconscious memories and the tag ends of daily consciousness. These took the form of the curious images he understood as an experience of "another country," since he did not dare to say "life after death."

But as crystal clear as the psychobiological explanation may appear to be, just as compelling are the considerations that the parapsychologists bring to the interpretation. They concede that the threshold point between life and death can vary from one individual to another. At the same time, they are unwilling to concede that contact with the afterworld represents only a failure of the brain to perform properly because of the malfunctioning of a group of thought cells.

Something more must be involved here besides a biologically grounded memory faculty in which everyday impressions have been distorted by the unconscious and the subconscious. It took more than this for the suicide of Red Square to tell about an experience he yearned to return to.

One time in Verona Dante was passing a house where several women were sitting in the doorway. One of them whispered: "Look at him! He goes to hell whenever he wants and comes back with news about the people down there!" "That's right," another said. "Just see how curly his beard is and how dark his skin. That comes from the heat and the smoke down there."

GIOVANNI BOCCACCIO (1313–1375)

12

"Volunteers Sought for Encounters with Death!"

HE IS DEAD NOW, beyond saving by anyone—properly dead like any human. Died in harness. Somewhere just across the Mexican border, at a place out of the reach of American detectives. He was done in by cirrhosis of the liver and allied ailments. Now, after his demise, what he experienced on the "other side," or is said to have experienced, is a story that can be told.

To be sure, he never of his own accord opened his mouth on the subject. But Dr. Robert E. Cornish was too interested in what this man was privy to. With a couple of pentothal and alcohol injections, he induced in him a state in which people begin to talk, inhibitions fall away and lips start to move, even if an inner voice says: You must keep still.

Thus this weird report came into being, a story that went the rounds among those acquainted with Dr. Cornish's experiments and whom he trusted enough to reveal sidelights of his practice which otherwise he preferred not to have mentioned in public.

For the man who died across the border in Mexico, and from whom Dr. Cornish, using truth serum, drew out things his subject wanted to keep hidden, had once sat in the electric chair. The man behind the curtain had thrown the high-voltage switch three times. Three times the current had hissed through him. In the death chamber, a former chapel, you could smell the stench of burned hair and seared flesh.

Believe it or not: He did indeed sit in this electric chair. Whoever says that no one can withstand a heavy current running between the copper headpiece and the leg clamps, since the brain cells would burn and boil away, simply does not know what a man like Fred Phillips was able to endure. Perhaps it was just the thickness of his skull, a skull so thick, strong, and bony at the coronal suture that one time before it had survived two pistol shots from rival bootleggers in the illicit moonshine trade.

Without this thick skull it is certain he would have never been able to live through electrocution. But whatever the reason for his survival, all that is important here is what he saw on the other side while the doctors in the execution chamber were writing out his death certificate:

"Death by electric current unqualifiedly confirmed. Release of the body authorized by special order of the Governor."

"I kept up my hopes to the last.

"They had smuggled notes into my cell saying: 'Don't give up. We'll get you out, man.'

"I believed in the guys who were sending me these promises. But how would they go about it? The guards outside were watching every minute. Nights one even sat with me in my cell. And no one ever came into this death row, this thicket of steel bars.

"I had read about Mata Hari. They told her that the firing squad would be using only blanks, so as to keep her strong for the last hour. They planted the hope in her that the whole thing would only turn out to be a comedy.

"Perhaps they were trying to keep up my hopes, too, so that I—Fred Phillips—would stick it out, *muy macho,* to the end.

"Anyway, I believed in my pals. I didn't realize it was all in vain until they came to take me away.

"It was all up then with the reprieve business. Any kind of release was out of the question. Now I was in the last room, from which I had only to step through one door to be in that other room. On the other side of the door I could hear them working around the big chair, getting it ready with wrenches and pliers.

"They came and took me in. They shaved the top of my head. Lower down they also shaved the hair off my legs and slit my shirtsleeve to lay my arm bare where the electrode would be strapped on.

"I ground my teeth—because I had been lied to, because they had raised hopes where there were none. But what to do about it now? Not one of them had come to say good-bye to me the last day. The guards told me this had never happened before.

"Now I was through the door and sitting in the chair. The black mask sank over my face. The metal hoops were fastened around my legs and arms. I felt the cold metal headpiece settle down on my head. I heard someone praying for me.

"I told them one last time that it wasn't me at all who had shot the four people in the garage that Thursday. I had only happened to be in the neighborhood. But I couldn't prove it— and that was why I was sitting in the electric chair, feeling the copper cap cold on my head, yesterday still covered with hair and now shaved bald, the better to conduct the current.

"They even powdered me at two places on my body, to keep the skin bone dry. For it had happened before that some people had broken out in such a sweat over the fear of dying that the current ran through the salty sweat instead of through the body, as it should. And getting it to run through my body was the whole idea of putting me into the electric chair.

"The man next to me seemed to be still praying, but his voice suddenly grew farther away. For a moment, indeed, he stopped altogether. It must have been that the man who even then was putting the black mask on me had signaled him to move back. Or given a sign to the man at the switch behind the curtain.

"Suddenly it happened.

"A panic of dread came over me—lasting just a moment— and I had never known panic before, not having any imagination. Never in all my life had I been terrified like this.

"But now suddenly this panic was on me, so enormous, so frightful, so agonizing that I could have roared from the pain and anguish of it. It was not the kind of pain you feel when you get a bullet in the leg, or if you're run over by a car, or take a beating.

"No, it was something different from that. I had the feeling that every cell in my body would explode, had to explode. Suddenly I felt myself getting big, swollen, as if I were three times bigger than in reality. I could feel the metal clasps biting into my flesh. The skin was taut under them.

"But anyway—I bellowed out of this terrible fear. I don't know whether they actually heard me or whether I was just screaming inside myself. In any case, I bellowed out, 'I will not die!'

"I kept on hollering this until suddenly I was in a completely green room, all alone, in a room that seemed to be lit up by the sun but which had no windows. And through one of the walls of this green space a creature came moving toward me.

"This figure was like a hairy giant of a man or an animal with a tremendous mouth and big slanting eyes.

"This thing walked up to me and reached out to grab me and set about strangling me to death. Yet, just before I had been just as much at home in the green room as a child might have been. And now I put up a battle against the colossus who was bent on throttling me. When he got very close, I noticed his hair smelled as if it had just been singed.

"Right away in this contest with the monster I knew I was going through all this business because actually I was dead.

"And I was afraid of being dead. Somehow I wasn't through with living yet. Now all was soon to be finished. I shouted out into the green space:

"'I want to live!'

"And every time I shouted like that, the walls shook, walls without any corners, round ones like the walls of a sphere. They shook every time I hollered and moved back a little from me.

"I yelled louder, louder, and louder, and wilder.

"Then I saw that the monster with the wide mouth and strange eyes was growing weaker under my hands, falling to pieces and shrinking all the time.

"I shouted and howled for my life and squashed the creature, now grown tiny, between my hands.

"The green sphere by now had become very wide—like a

cathedral dome. I sat in the middle of this broadness and hollered for my life.

"Then the green sphere began to turn—slowly at first, then faster, and finally went so fast that I got dizzy and had to shut my eyes. I couldn't open them again. And yet all the while I wanted to see the peaceful green color and the tremendous dome of light that was still around me.

"I wasn't seeing the green color any more—nor the dome.

"But in my eyes, which were now looking into blackness, darkness, sparks seemed to be coming at me from far off. They kept coming closer and turned into tongues of flame.

"However, I was not afraid at all of this fire coming at me.

"Finally I heard voices, people's voices, hurriedly whispering directions to one another. I tried to understand what these voices had to do with me, someone who was dead like me. Were they against me? I heard 'Hold the rubber basin a little higher. The water could be a little warmer, too.'

"'Massage him harder. Always work from the bottom up!'

"'Fasten on those electrodes! Put one on his chest, the other on his neck—still higher—so the shock of the current will hit directly into the occipital cavity!'

"'He's not moving. It's not working. Fred's dead.'

"Then it must be all about me, what they's saying. They were talking about me. They were taking care of me. But although I could hear them, I wasn't feeling anything.

"They'd said that Fred was dead. Yet I definitely was hearing them talking. If I could hear them talking, I couldn't be dead, even though I had just been feeling that I was, sitting inside the big green dome.

"Had I really died? Was I hearing voices although I seemed no longer to have a body? It seemed to me as if I was nothing but a head—a head without a trunk. Really, not even a head. For otherwise I would have been able to move my lips and say something.

"I was only a brain. I was only a thought, an idea. But I could hear thoughts and react to the beams of light shooting at me.

"All of a sudden I felt I was lying in a car, a car that was traveling cross-country, racing over a badly paved road, as it seemed to me. I felt the jolts when the wheels bumped over potholes. That was the first physical feeling I had.

"'We've got to give him another injection.'

"The voice didn't say 'heart injection,' but now I noticed that I had a heart. The needle went right through my ribs—and into my heart. From this point on it seemed that the feeling of being alive, of having a body—the sensation I had lacked a few moments ago—was beginning to come back to me.

"I had it made! I was alive again. The feeling of being alive kept on growing, out from my heart. Pretty soon my chin had come back. I could bite my teeth together. But I still had no torso, or any arms or legs. It was a long time before I became a human being again.

"And the vehicle in which I was riding kept on racing across the countryside, over a badly paved road.

"Suddenly I was able to open my eyes. Leaning over me I saw a man wearing big glasses with heavy rims. He had a piercing look. He wore a white cap, the kind doctors put on during operations. The face under the glasses was covered with a white cloth.

"I tried to turn my head to see what was happening.

"'Don't move yet! Stay perfectly still!' the man with the heavy-rimmed glasses hissed at me.

"But I could barely move in any case. The ride was a terrible ordeal for me. I told that to the man bending over me. From under his mask he shouted something to the driver. Apparently the driver then pulled off the highway and turned into a dirt road to stop there.

"I thought that I was lying in an ambulance. But was it really an ambulance? It looked more like a hearse, one of the finest, the kind supplied by the best American funeral parlors.

"I'd ridden in a hearse like that once, the time we took little Johnny to the crematorium after he'd been killed for not showing up at the boss's with all that money he was supposed to deliver.

"It was because of that I recognized the hearse from the inside. Two of us had gone along with the casket to do the honors. One of the two had been me.

"But what had they made out of this hearse? A chemical lab, a medical center, with glittering tubes and water containers on the walls, all sorts of flasks and pumps and rubber tubes.

"An operating room in a hearse! That's what they'd changed the inside into.

"And now the people in the hearse had brought me back to life.

"'You did come after all,' I whispered to one of the people who were at one side of me and who also wore masks over their faces that left only their eyes free. By their eyes I knew these men were not doctors, but our own people.

"The men with the hard eyes only nodded. What was there for them to say? The boss had given orders that the famous Dr. X was to be called and then they had arranged everything else. It had cost a lot of loot to get influential senators to pressure the governor into releasing Fred Phillips's dead body. But they had managed to do it.

"And so it happened that I was now alive again.

"But—when I'm alone and shut my eyes—then I try to remember again and again all about the green place that arched over me like a dome. And I'm afraid of the monster with the big mouth and the sloping eyes, even though I could crush the thing to bits with my hands . . ."

Fred Phillips talked about the green cathedral dome for the rest of his life. Dr. X was asked about it on a few occasions, since it was believed Phillips was suffering from an *idée fixe*, the first stages of a mental illness, or something of the sort. But Dr. X only shook his head, saying:

"Nobody ever gets over an experience like that. Best thing is to forget about his cranium. It may be that under the impact of the electric current a few brain cells here and there were glued together and from this came the idea of being in a gigantic green room. In other words, to some extent the notion could come from a cerebral anomaly that he is able to tolerate.

Let's leave him alone with his memory of the green cathedral space."

Fred Phillips had been robust enough to make it through despite everything. It was not until the very end of it, when he was living in Mexico—where he had gone to keep it quiet that he was not dead—that he began to drink heavily. He drank because at night he could not get rid of the monster who smelled of burned hair.

This drinking led to cirrhosis of the liver. And it was cirrhosis of the liver that killed Phillips. Even Dr. X could not help him this time.

It has never been proved that Dr. Cornish was the Dr. X who brought Fred Phillips back from eternity. Certainly, a man like Dr. Cornish would never admit to reviving a man sentenced to death by a state court and duly executed. His scientific reputation and his freedom to carry on scientific work would be jeopardized. And the famous Dr. Cornish's experiments are recognized not only in the United States but abroad.

First to attract notice were Dr. Cornish's experiments on dogs. He claimed to be able to revive animals dead for ten days by using a common kitchen-salt solution of strongly vitalizing effect. He stipulated, of course, that the moment the animals were dead they had to be put in a cold room to prevent decomposition. His famous experiment with the fox terrier Lazarus II was widely discussed. Lazarus II was anesthetized with oxygen and ether. After six minutes his heart stopped beating. The doctor then opened one of the apparently dead animal's veins and injected a salt solution saturated with oxygen and also containing a large amount of adrenalin, a liver extract, and a little canine blood from which the coagulating components had been extracted.

After this treatment Lazarus II was put aside in the cold room. And it was from this cold room that they took him out and began to blow oxygen into his mouth, to massage him and impart a rocking motion to his body. The result was that after a few minutes the dog's legs began to twitch. Then his heart started to beat. For eighteen hours and thirteen minutes

Lazarus hovered in a dreadful state between life and death. He whimpered, breathed, and moved. But when he was injected with a glucose solution in the hope of keeping life in his body, Lazarus II stretched out and this time was forever dead.

Why was it that Dr. Cornish carried out such experiments? His teacher had been Dr. George Washington Crile. Forty years earlier Dr. Crile had mooted the possibility of bringing dead creatures back to life. This led to Dr. Cornish's having had word passed around that he was looking for volunteers for experiments with death. He offered the assurance that he would bring them back to life after fifteen minutes with the aid of his salt solution.

Among all Cornish's experiments, or at least the ones the world knows about, undoubtedly the one with Fred Phillips is the most remarkable. It is not known for a fact, to be sure, that Cornish was the man with the piercing eyes behind the thick-rimmed glasses, that is, whether he was the Dr. X who, sub rosa, carried out the experiment of reviving an executed criminal.

Let me linger in that land of harmony and justice.
So that I shall not be abandoned
To aloneness; for now I have become a citizen
Of a universe where the eye, grown dim,
Sees nothing. An is my name . . .
O, could I but tarry among the holy spirits
Complete and mighty!

Egyptian Book of the Dead, Chapter 13

13

Three Weeks in the Beyond

"AND YOU'VE GIVEN UP ALL HOPE, DOCTOR?"

"By human standards—yes. You know, in these fever attacks, a certain point is the limit. If you go beyond it, the patient's body, his blood, can't offer enough resistance. He's done for."

"But Mrs. Theresa Laffeld has had several attacks when her temperature rose as high as one hundred and eighteen degrees. Yet she lived through them and afterward was perfectly well. In any case, relative to the physical condition that is causing these fevers—"

"Exceptions, pure exceptions. Accidents I'm still not able to account for. You know that with normal people there can be temperatures as high as one hundred and nine. In malaria even a little higher. But anything over that means death. The spark of life is extinguished.

"I've got about forty years of practice behind me. Twice I've seen temperatures of up to one hundred eleven. But beyond that—death. The blood simply begins to coagulate. I've experienced it in practice myself three times."

"Yes, but Mrs. Laffeld isn't dead yet. She's still alive! And we calibrated the thermometer especially for this case. There can't be a mistake."

"You're right. Mrs. Laffeld is a sensation. This young woman is a phenomenon just to have lived to be twenty-six years old. Theoretically, she should have been dead long ago. But instead, for all practical purposes she dies twice a week—and keeps on living. I suspect that this strange endocarditis she's suffering from is giving rise to processes in her body we don't know about. Maybe they explain these rapid temperature changes."

"And how do you think the end will come?"

"Rather suddenly when it happens. Over the long run, the blood, like the rest of the body, cannot endure insults that are beyond all human capacity.

"I suspect this half coming back to consciousness will cease gradually. She will then lapse into a coma, a continuing sleep state, during which these powerful fever attacks will continue and mortally undermine the organism."

Professor Johns, who as chief of staff at the hospital in Whitechapel, London, was responsible for Theresa Laffeld, seemed to be right in his prognosis during the next few days. Mrs. Laffeld, who should have been long dead, sank between fever attacks into a sort of paralysis that at times took on the character of tetany.

"One day she's going to die in her sleep right under our noses. You might say she's practically dead right now. She doesn't react any more. She's just barely breathing, and having those fever crises by themselves should have killed her by now."

But presently the whole picture changed. The fever attacks stopped. They began to believe there might be a miracle after all. This miracle became reality.

One day Theresa Laffeld opened her eyes—and in bewilderment asked what day it was. Actually, she had been on the other side for weeks—dead for three weeks—absolutely dead.

"All this time, what were you dreaming about, what did you hear and see? Or was everything dark? Did you just sleep?"

For a long time Mrs. Laffeld stared at the doctor who was questioning her, then turned her face to the wall. The doctor dropped the subject, realizing that the woman either did not want to talk or was unable to. Twice he had seen people reawaken from the dead—once a drunkard, once a man who had been hanged. And neither had had anything to say. But these two other people had been on "the other side" for only a few minutes. With this woman it was three weeks. The doctor couldn't get over it. He had to know more. He would have to draw it out of her.

He phoned an old friend who worked in a West End psychiatric clinic and asked his advice.

"An interesting case. You know, I think I'll come over to your place. Mind if I'm there? When the patient is strong enough, we'll give her an injection to induce an artificial hypnosis. It will affect only a portion of the brain while allowing us to penetrate the movements of the subconscious, if we wish, and beyond that it will clearly release the capacity to remember.

"I'll be over tonight around ten. Tell your patient it has to do with a checkup, to brain waves, or something of the sort. Say we want to test how well her psychological activity has been normalized. You have to offer the patient at least some explanation."

"But do we have the right to carry out this experiment? And ask her questions?"

"Whatever we find we can keep to ourselves as long as we live. Or, at any rate, as long as the woman lives. That's up to us. We'll have kept our vow of confidentiality and at the same time served science . . ."

"Breathe very slowly, Theresa—breathe evenly. You are Theresa Laffeld, twenty-six years old, born in Manchester.

"I'm asking you to remember what happened to you, what you saw and heard, when you were dead to the world for three weeks. Try to recall everything.

"What did you see first when you went to sleep? Three weeks ago, when you didn't wake up any more after the fever attack of January twenty-third."

In her artificially induced hypnotic sleep, the patient seemed to be suffering torments stemming from something in her that opposed talking. But the psychiatrist's commands became more peremptory. He wanted to know all.

"Theresa Laffeld! You're going to talk to me. Remember! Speak up!"

Theresa's lips began to move. She was unable to resist the

orders the man was giving her, urgings that echoed in her brain like military commands.

"I got younger all the time. All of a sudden I wasn't twenty-six years old any more, but a young girl. And then I got younger still. I was a child, a tiny little child. I was playing in my mother's lap. But then I seemed to start melting away. I became even tinier. And then . . ."

"Think back, Theresa! There's more to it than that. That's just the beginning. You were very small. Everything around you was dark. You weren't even born yet. But what was there before that? Where did you come from into the darkness inside your mother?"

"I was a very old man, dying. No, I was already dead. But I hadn't found any peace because even when I was alive I'd been so restless . . . always roaming through the world. At that time . . . when I was living as a man . . . I was called John Clavel.

"I had a very hard death. A very hard departure from this world. No doubt because I'd been so mean—especially with a woman. This woman had come to me when she was very young and I was already a very old man. She loved me and I mistreated her. Yes, that's the way I was—John Clavel!

"When I was young—you know, I lived through this whole life backward, not from birth to death, but from death to birth. How did it go then? When I was very young, I enlisted in some branch or other of the army. I traveled over the water—and therefore . . ."

"Do you hear me, John Clavel? John! You've got to speak out. Don't try to give us the slip!"

"Yes, I have to speak. When I was dead, I looked for a woman who would bear a child, and then I found the mother of this girl—this Theresa Laffeld.

"And when I was young, very young—I was living somewhere on the Continent. I had a mother who'd been abandoned by a man. On account of me, when everything around me was dark, she cried a lot. I heard this crying though I was still in the dark . . ."

"John Clavel! What was there before that darkness that was

all around you? There was something before that, wasn't there? You've got to remember."

"A very old woman who said mean things about people sat in a little stone house and wanted to die. But right to the last minute she hated everything and everybody.

"That was my changeover from darkness to another person who died.

"Yes, I was mean. I was called Philomene Carter.

"I hated people the way they hated me. Once I had been pretty, like other young women. But the man I loved left me in the lurch because someone else was richer. And I carried this hatred with me to the end. Why should I be nice to people after they did me nothing but harm!

"I was very beautiful . . . but that was long ago . . . It's more than . . . I can't keep track of the years any more. But . . ."

"Feel the patient's pulse!"

"Too fast. We've got to be careful. I've noticed that when she gets to transitions, to her existence between two lives, the phase separating any two periods, that the patient reacts very strongly."

"Yes, we'd better break it off for today. Perhaps some other time we'll have another chance to continue with this amazing descent into the past of a person who seems to have had many lives.

"But now we'd better let her sleep quietly. Stay with her, say, another hour or so. Then we'll try to wake her up. Meanwhile, I'll be in the lab. I want to look over our encephalogram recordings."

Then, later . . .

"Hasn't she come to yet?"

"I've looked over the encephalograms. Never seen anything like them. At first nothing but alpha waves, then a sudden transition to beta ones, then all of a sudden there are places on the film as if they'd been lightstruck by a flashlight—a very faint circle, like the aura around a foggy sun . . ."

"It must have happened exactly at those transition points we were just talking about, when the pulse became so irregular."

Both doctors wrote up detailed reports on this experience.
They were unable to continue the experiment because the
patient, showing a stubbornness like never before, asked the
next day to be released from the hospital. She would not tell
the doctor why she wanted to leave. She would hardly look
at him. Yet she was unaware, all this time, of what had happened to her during her artificially induced hypnosis.

She vanished from the hospital and from London. When,
some time later, the doctor and his psychiatrist friend went
looking for her, they could not find a trace of her. Thus, all
that remains are these interesting notes on a person who for
three weeks was in another world. Nothing but fragments—
fragments like all the others, attempts, against the subjects'
will, to capture on recording paper, tape, phonographic disk,
or stenographer's pad the experiences of people who have
come all too close to the brink of the beyond.

The Whitechapel doctor who undertook, for his personal
and scientific satisfaction, to evaluate the condition of his patient Theresa Laffeld naturally was not the first to think of the
possibility of forcing people to reveal deep memories while
sick, dying, or narcoleptic.

"It doesn't matter whether or not we believe in rebirth,
reincarnation, or metempsychosis, it's still worth noting that
all such experiments yield one common result: People recall
earlier existences."

This is the opinion of the famous psychiatrist Dr. William
Cannon, who carried out unique psychological experiments,
a series of investigations that lay outside all ordinary psychology, while not obtruding into the still ill-defined realm of parapsychology.

Cannon, too, worked on people's recall back into the time
before birth. He used all sorts of people in these experiments.
It was unaccountable but demonstrable that with many subjects recall failed after going back to the third year. And yet,
with others it was readily possible to penetrate, by probing
backward, into the time before birth.

"When I put people like this into a trancelike state and forced them to think back, the film of their experience was simply projected backward. And if I was lucky enough to penetrate even further, then the exposition began with a description of an old person who gradually became younger."

This parallels the results of the doctors' experiment at the Whitechapel hospital. However, Dr. Cannon discovered—after in one case working his way back through no less than six lives and arriving at a seventh—that beyond a certain point something peculiar occurred, later confirmed many times in repeat experiments, something that none but he has ever demonstrated.

Before the seventh life, or in the transition from an earlier eighth life, or out of nothingness to a seventh life, a "band" appeared: a band of light between the unknown, that is, nothingness, that led or guided the subject into his seventh life. In the seventh life he floated or soared as if he had wings, as if for him the force of gravity no longer existed. By contrast, moreover, all previous existences had been marked by the same struggles with suffering and care that are familiar in all daily lives; for earthbound people lacking a Dr. Cannon or some other psychiatrist to transpose them back into another world, at the most, release can only be dreamed about, but never known about in waking life.

No, never known about, any more than the people who were hypnotized by Dr. Cannon could afterward remember what they had told him about their earlier existences while under narcosynthesis.

"But for the parapsychologist it is important to point out that these people's descriptions always run backward but never forward—run backward into that mysterious existence where the soul of someone almost dead must tarry, as it were. It could well be that the people recruited for these experiments were nearer to death than the doctors believed, and that what came out during their apparently deathlike sleep was nothing more than a recall of previous existences, a looking back that perhaps at a certain point would have had to end up in genuine death . . .

"In any event, from these descriptions of deep memories of

earlier lives we can draw the conclusion that they sound quite different from what has been told by people of whom it can be said that they died and came back from the dead.

"This protracted dying, this slow and contemplative lingering on the brink between this and the other side, obviously does not give the soul seeking a way out the possibility of a flight really leading to the far shore. Yet these experiences come very close to it. There must be only a thin dividing line between them. That band of light that binds evolving creatures with nothingness—either with nothingness or some other previous existence—is also found in many accounts from people who have been near death. And this band of light may be the tie between what we otherwise know of the hereafter and what people tell us who believe they have been in the after-world for days or weeks."

This is the parapsychologist's evaluation of these events. Naturally, there is a difference between having the barriers torn down by sleep, genuine or induced, and that other great happening, greatest of all after being born: the experience of death. But things do touch each other. They are related above all in the behavior of those who have such experiences to report. Their lips are shut fast. They look off toward the wall. Only by the medical magic of narcoanalytic drugs can they be induced, in a curious state of half-sleep, to tell in whispers about what was out there between this and the other world.

≈§¦≈

"You are now standing before the god of death!"

In vain you will try to deny your evil deeds. In the supreme judge's mirror appear all the figures involved in your dealings. Know this, that all the shapes that you can see in the post-mortem state, named *bardo*, are unreal; they are dream images conjured up by yourself and you are sending them forth without recognizing them as your own handiwork, and they terrify you. The mirror, in which the judge of the dead seems to be reading, is your own conscience, reminding you of the chain of events which he is judging according to concepts shaped by yourself; that is, according to your own ideas of good and evil. You are the one who pronounces judgment; no dreadful god drives you to it. For know this: Other than your own metaphysical projections, there are neither gods nor demons, nor any judge of the dead—not even the so-called *bardo*. Understand this at last and be free.

BARDO THÖDOL (the *Tibetan Book of the Dead*, in the original version of Padma Sambhava, c. A.D. 749)

14

In the Cave of
the Dead

SVEN STEFFENSON had always been a loner. Even when the day
came that he could see his way to make the long trip through
Tibet, he did not join up with an expedition. He went by himself to try to get to the bottom of secrets he had longed to un-
ravel since earliest youth.

Anyone who ventures alone into the mountains of the Himalayas must count on the treacherous surprises that nature holds
in readiness for the foolhardy. The Tibetans, indeed, believe
that the vengeance of the gods, who want their mountains un-
touched, will descend on those who undertake to pry into their
mysteries.

One day Sven Steffenson, an outstanding mountain climber,
had a sudden fall in the Himalayas. He hurtled down steep
slopes and scree for a distance of nearly five thousand feet.

He was found by Tibetan tea smugglers on the way from
China. There was still a spark of life left in him. And because
a cave monastery was located so nearby, they took him along
and left him there.

It was in this way that Sven Steffenson found himself in
the "Cave of the Dead." This Tibetan cave has been called this
for centuries, for it is believed that the cave is haunted by the
spirits of thousands of the dead.

The Tibetan monks who live in the cave seem, with time,
to have developed an insensitivity to these things. They end-
lessly chant their monotonous prayer texts about the sweet
mystery of the lotus bud and pay no attention to the ghosts

who rise about them, who walk with them to prayer, or who pray in rhythms unfamiliar even to the monks.

Steffenson lay in the Cave of the Dead for six long months with a broken back, strapped up so he was unable to move and tended to keep the spark of life in him alive.

An English expedition transporting a lighting installation to Lhasa passed near the Cave of the Dead. One of the monks told them a white man was lying in the cave. And so it happened that after they had delivered their consignment at the next high pass to a Tibetan transport column, the Englishmen took Sven Steffenson along with them on their way back.

He was paralyzed, a pitiful cripple, and had to be handled carefully as he was carried over the mountains, since the least movement caused him horrible pain. Steffenson spent almost two years in a hospital in northern India. He then died a miserable death, having passed beyond the power of anyone to help. But before he died, he dictated everything he had seen and felt in the Cave of the Dead.

"I think I was more dead than alive after that terrible fall. But today I remember everything, I can recall it all exactly.

"I had gone too far out on an out-thrust of rock. The rock gave way under me without warning. I suddenly realized I was falling. I reached out here and there as I fell, automatically trying to grab hold of something. Thoughts and images of extraordinary precision and clarity flashed through my mind. I considered the consequences of the fall. I resolved that as soon as I landed somewhere I would take my little alcohol flask out of my pocket and have a shot to keep up my vital spirits. It went through my head that I was wearing glasses and the splinters of glass could get into my eyes if the lenses shattered in the fall.

"Suddenly it occurred to me that the book I had intended to write about my journey would never be completed if I were killed.

"I dreamed even as I was falling. I thought thousands of things and was unafraid. Then suddenly I felt a muffled blow, a crash, but with no pain. No, I had no pain—nor any feeling of horror, or lack of breath.

"Then I felt myself slipping and sliding again and once more I was floating in space.

"Only now I was looking up into the sky as I fell. I saw the clouds and between the clouds a wonderful patch of blue arching over the mountain peaks. And I kept on falling and sliding. It amazed me that I should have no pain.

"Then came a heavy, dull crash as I came to a stop. I never did get to drink a slug from the little flask, for I had lost consciousness. Or more than that?

"I was lying right in the middle of a gigantic dark vault. Not another creature was there. This vaulted place was icy cold. I saw huge birds flapping down toward me from the roof of the place. They came very close and had enormous round eyes that flashed when they were real close to me, as if they had fire in them. These birds were as big as I was. They could have been bats. But are there such gigantic bats?

"I wondered, seeing these creatures, if I was dead. I felt no fear of the birds, and the coolness of the vault felt comfortable to me.

"More and more birds circled around me. Then fireflies came. They hung above my head like tiny lanterns, then moved a little to the right and a little to the left, after which they shot down a way toward me, only to fly away again.

"I knew I couldn't move, but I had no pain. I certainly had to be dead.

"If I shut my eyes, everything began to turn around—in any case, I had the feeling that whatever equilibrium a dead man might have left would be shattered if I didn't keep my eyes fixed on the monstrous bats and the lightning bugs. But can a dead man close his eyes in the first place?

"One day—or one night—anyway, after spending many days in this dark, cool, vaulted place, suddenly figures appeared carrying torches and wearing masks on their heads. They turned my blood cold. Frightful eyes goggled at me. Creatures without anything human left about them circled about me and swiped at me with their torches, but without hitting me, like skilled acrobats who knew how to dance and dodge over me with a lightness, a wingedness, that had nothing mortal left about it.

"After this weird visitation from the creatures with the disguises and the masks, the torches and the glowing firebrands, I suddenly saw the first Tibetan monks with their shaven heads, the people who had taken me in and were caring for me.

"I don't remember how long I must have lain there. I don't know whether I'd been dead before and now had been brought back to life, or what it was that had happened to me.

"In any case, when the monks went away and I was alone again, the apparitions, the bats, and the big fireflies came back and played their games with me in my helplessness and defenselessness. And yet I had no fear, just as I had no pain.

"There was not a soul to talk to, because the monks who visited me never spoke. One day they brought me into another cave. This one wasn't as dark, and was warmer than the giant one that had seemed like a gigantic dome to me. In the smaller cave I experienced a thousandfold what Dante imagined on his journey into hell. Why had they brought me there?

"Here there were no more giant bats swooping down on me. Now it was people, or, more exactly, creatures that had once been people, who came coiling about me. I tried to grab at them, but my hands refused to function. The figures came very close and shone through the darkness. They had transparent bodies. Their hands were bony, as if the skin and flesh had fallen away from them, but their bodies were still intact—or in any case had contour. Except that you could see right through them.

"They came and reached out to me and stroked me. I shuddered under the touch of their ice-cold hands.

"Forms that perhaps had once been women bent over me and kissed me on the mouth. I lay in a swoon of fear and could do nothing against these ghosts from the Cave of the Dead.

"In all events, when the spookiness faded away, when it grew quieter around me—that is, whenever the monks would suddenly materialize out of nowhere into a protective circle about me, against which the ghosts were powerless—at these

times of reprieve I tried to collect my thoughts. I tried to keep
my senses, to keep rational track of everything, to convince myself that I must be having delirious dreams caused by the fall
in the mountains, for my memory of that had come back.

"Perhaps this circling about me of spirits and the ghosts of
the dead had made me go off my rocker for a time, short or
long. Then you people came along to take me out of it.

"I don't know whether you heard it or not. But when you
were taking me out of the cave—my own ears had got used to
the sounds in that weird world—I caught the screeching and
the mocking titters of the spirits. They didn't like losing their
plaything, their helpless toy, a bit . . ."

The autopsy on Sven Steffenson revealed that he had sustained a double fracture of the skull in his plunge down the
mountain. A double fracture, and in addition two spinal frac-
tures, in themselves usually enough to kill a man in a few hours.
But the Tibetans are said to understand how to deal with such
injuries extraordinarily well—except that ordinarily they would
never use their finest skills on a white man whose aims and
intentions they could not grasp. Nonetheless, they did not let
him die.

They did not use pitchblende on him. Pitchblende lies hidden in the deepest gorges and caves of the Himalayas, pitchblende shot through with radioactive materials that can heal
breaks, it is said, in short order.

A double skull fracture, the spinal column broken in two
places, complete paralysis, apparently a very high fever—all
these things, says the English report on Sven Steffenson's fall,
would suffice to give rise to hallucinations in this curious individual's brain, already teeming with Tibetan cultist mysteries.

In a man who had suffered such injuries and shock, damag-
ing the retina or the visual centers of the brain, it is unquestionably possible for visual delusions to arise. For example,
the disturbances can take the form of an enormous enlargement of percept images. Bats typically fluttering about in caves
become giant bats. Sparks arising from retinal stimuli, quite
without benefit of lightning bugs, can glare like incandescent
lamps in the visual center.

The figures with the masks and firebrands in every way bring to mind the devil-dancers found all the way from Ceylon to Mongolia. These dancers try, by shock effect, to reverse sickness. Why should not the Tibetans, interested in saving this white man, have turned to devil-dancers when he was hovering between life and death? On other occasions they use them in a joint effort to mobilize gods and devils.

The hallucinations in the Cave of the Dead, the English account goes on to say, may be explained on the basis of certain light effects, by the damp mists that can occur in these cases due to temperature and humidity changes. If a deathly sick person is harassed and upset by long solitude and the uncertainty of his fate, it is easy to understand how the cave fogs might assume shapes in his brain, shapes that would accord with ideas already present thanks to mystical predilection.

This is the matter-of-fact interpretation of the experiences of this strange pilgrim to Tibet, who for a brief span was snatched from the jaws of death.

However, if the Tibetan monks themselves were asked for their opinions on dying and life after death, and their interpretation of the case of Sven Steffenson, and their attitude toward reports of clinical death, what they would have to say would probably reflect their tremendously old monastery traditions.

The *Tibetan Book of the Dead* provides a comprehensive explanation of post-mortem experiences during the *bardo*, or astral state between death and rebirth in the concept of Lamaism. In this state there are, symbolically, forty-nine days until rebirth. The instructions provided the deceased for his sojourn in the afterworld are divided into three segments, and politely suggest rather than firmly command what should be done.

The first part describes the experiences, the events, the behavior of the psyche at the moment of death. After definitive death, we are told, comes a dream state fraught with illusions that become ever more gloomy and horrible the closer the deceased gets to rebirth.

The ancient Egyptians, as clearly shown in their *Book of the*

Dead, believed that the deceased does not arrive within view of the god of light and truth until he has completed his journey through the underworld and the heavenly spheres. In contrast, the Buddhists believe that the transition into the beyond entails "complete illumination." With his lips pressed to the dying man's ear, the lama or monk continuously intones prayers so that the stricken man will concentrate his thoughts absolutely on the great experience confronting him. When the last breath is drawn, the prayer leader says:

"O, noble born, hearken. Now you are experiencing the radiance of the clear light, of pure reality. Recognize it. O, noble born, your now existing spirit [the ability to know or to perceive], empty now of its actual nature, not formed to be something having features or color, empty in a natural sense, is the true reality, the all-beneficent mother.

"Your proper spirit, that is now emptiness, is not, however, to be regarded as the emptiness of nothingness, but as pure spirit, untrammeled, radiant, responsive, and happy, and is the true consciousness, the all-beneficent Buddha [father]."

According, then, to Buddhist teachings, this afterdeath consciousness is radiant, empty, and incorporated within the great body of radiance that is the final source. This last is light primeval, unchanging, and knows neither birth nor death. Awareness of these things permits the departed to abide within the bosom of the divine spirit. Time is not a decisive factor in the process of revelation. The loss of consciousness can last a few minutes or as much as three or four days.

The instructions read by the lama for the second and third stages of the *bardo* interlude are aimed, therefore, at making the dying attentive not only to the delusions, the entanglements, and the possibility of release from them that can come at any moment, but also at serving to explain the nature of illusions.

Take, for example, the Tibetan court of the dead, a concept with analogues in the Egyptian religion and in Christianity as the Last Judgment. According to Buddhist theology, the central figure in the vision of a court of the dead is Dharma-Raja, king of truth. Dharma-Raja has a third eye in the middle of his forehead, and the flames of truth burn about him. Since he is also the god of death, he holds in his right hand the sword of spiritual dominion and in his left the mirror of karma (principle of causality determining future existence), in which the good and evil deeds of the dead are reflected. The scales are held by an ape-headed god, flanked by two other gods, one with a head like a bull, the other like a snake. These last two superintend the weighing, for which black and white pebbles are used. Passing the examination, which can stretch over a period of time for which there is no worldly measure, depends on the moral character of the departed.

Whereas other religions do not go beyond the court-of-justice notion, in Buddhism there are additional visions, also governed by thought forms and action from the living world. The fearsome god of anger appears to a person of violent temper, the hideous god of avarice to a miser. There are hosts of blood-drinking gods with misplaced limbs and twisted bodies who instill fear and terror into the dead.

The recapitulation of physical existence proceeds in step with these visions and ends in reincarnation and rebirth.

Alexandra David-Neel, the French orientalist who died in 1868, centered her investigations on Buddhism. Among her posthumous papers she left behind an interesting conversation with the Dalai Lama of Tibet. Among other things, the following was said:

"Do Christians, though they follow the religion of Issu [Jesus], also go to *bardo* when they die?"

"Certainly!"

"But they don't believe in the gods of lamaism, or in reincarnation, or in anything written in the *Bardo Thödol.*"

"They will still go to *bardo.* However, what they see there will be Issu, angels, paradise, hell, and the like. In their projecting spirit they will see all the things they have been taught which they believe in. They will have visions which in some cases will frighten them, for instance, the Last Judgment, the torments of hell. Their images and experiences during their dream journey will be different from a Tibetan's. But in essence it will be the same thing. The psychomental impressions stored up during the individual's lifetime will take on forms and be represented as ensouled images. Thus the Tibetan, the Christian, or any other disembodied being will tend to view these visions as real events unfolding in the form of a series of thoughts."

However this interpretation of the experiences of Sven Steffenson may sound, let us now return to the United States, where yet another person apparently dead—indeed, already buried—also had something to relate about her temporary sojourn in the beyond.

Many years ago Mrs. Anna Lee died on a stormy afternoon just after a hurricane had swept over the region. She had been ill for a long time with an ailment the doctors were unable to diagnose, but it must have entailed psychic disturbances that greatly weakened the heart.

Mrs. Lee was buried in the family vault in a glass-covered coffin. The second day after her burial, the cemetery caretaker, going by the vault, heard a weak, plaintive voice. The caretaker stood still. Could he have been mistaken? No, the voice called out a second time. Terrified, the man ran out of the cemetery and fetched a doctor. He had no desire to go alone to the casket from which he had heard the voice coming.

When the doctor and the caretaker opened the coffin, they found that Mrs. Lee had become conscious again. She was removed to a hospital, and fifteen days later was fit to be released. Two years after this incident, she gave birth to a child. Meanwhile, she said repeatedly that she had only been given a temporary reprieve from the afterlife. She was in the world of the living on furlough, as it were.

"When others say they have seen shapes and talked to creatures in the afterworld, they must have been in a different one from the one I was in. All I know is that I was in a great, reddish-brown vault. I had the feeling that this vault, this sphere, was someone's head—or brain. In any case, I felt safely hidden and very happy in this dark space. Yet suddenly I realized—perhaps this huge brain or head had thought it— that I couldn't stay where I was. Through me, in me, someone wanted to find a way out of the beyond back into the mortal world. Because of this I came back and gave birth to this child.

"I won't live much longer now. The child will go the way ordained for it in the other world. I was only a means to an end."

When Mrs. Lee died of a heart attack a year after the birth of her child, an autopsy revealed that, by rights, physiologically speaking, she should have been dead years ago. For the mysterious influences that enabled her to overcome death, even the sensible physiologists could offer no reasons.

We might speculate that this woman with the sickly body had had a tremendously strong will to live and that she had used this will in her fight against physical deterioration. Not until her will had achieved expression in a reincarnation—that is, a child—had she considered her role in life to be completed. And then she died a second time—this time for good.

How close this gravely ill woman came to the threshold between this world and the next can hardly be judged from her own account. People who have taken mind-distorting drugs, drugs that could have been present in the medicine given Mrs. Lee, often report the sensation of having their brains expand into domes or vaults.

In this manner, notions could have evolved in her brain that broke through the barriers of normal thought and feeling in her quest for fulfillment.

❧❦❧

If you have lost possession of a world, do not be filled with pain about it, it is nothing.

If you have won possession of a world, do not rejoice about it, it is nothing.

Pains and pleasures pass, so pass the world by, it is nothing.

Awari Soheili (Persian poet,
as cited by Schopenhauer)

15

Excursions into Various Spheres

THESE PEOPLE HAVE SAID they came back from the dead, from paradise, from another world. But there are also people among us who, to a degree, are able on their own initiative to undertake expeditions to the "other side," and after the completion of their curious journey tell us about what they have seen and felt.

Nature endowed Helen Aintree with this extraordinary gift. Mrs. Aintree, who lives in Southsea, England, is sound of health and in full possession of her faculties. She is not one of the many mediums who regard themselves as a nexus between the everyday world and the supernatural world, whose body is taken over during a trance by the spirit of a dead person, thus permitting the spirit to talk to the living.

To this good-looking, lively woman of forty-eight, a trip to the land of the dead is easier than traveling on earth from one big city to the next.

Many friends, and strangers as well, come to her for a sign from dead relatives.

The Reverend Andrew Woolcott is a longtime friend. He notes that her descriptions of the other world can also be found, differently worded, in the Bible. He says:

"I'm convinced that Helen can and does take trips into the beyond. What she describes tallies completely with similar reports by many prominent psychic investigators."

People already convinced that death is not the final end naturally put this question to her: "What's it like, the place I'll have to go to when my heart stops beating?"

Helen Aintree gives this answer:

"It's a place of peace and quiet where earthly care and struggle, earthly suffering and misery, have no meaning. It is a land of lovely hills and valleys, of splendid golden cities and smiling faces.

"The light there is not the glaring sunlight that we know. Rather, it seems to come from everywhere. It's more like a kind of glow or radiance emanating from everyone and everything.

"The air is filled with curious sounds—with a music unlike anything ever composed by a human being. It is the music of nature, speaking in a voice intelligible to all.

"We have heard, of course, of the basic 'harmony of nature.' Now, there you can actually apprehend it, as a glorious music. Laughter and warmth radiate everywhere. There is no envy and no struggle for existence, since everyone has what he had been striving for. Time does not obtain there in our conception of it, only the everlasting and eternal witness of the power of love."

The reason why Helen Aintree herself does not need to die to reach this other land she explains as follows:

"An essential part of the human substance is imperishable. We call it the soul. Death separates the immortal soul from the body to bring it to the higher spheres where it really belongs.

"If these higher spheres really exist, I cannot see why dying should be the only way of reaching them. All that is needed is a tremendous desire and intensity of spirit. And the power of the spirit is unimaginable.

"In the world of peace, which lies in wait for all of us, we have the possibility of creating a state of being susceptible, to a certain extent, to being fashioned by our own wishes. There we receive guidance and help in reaching the spiritual goals for which we long. A composer may create a kind of music in the hereafter beyond his scope on earth. A painter may be able to paint in a way beyond his previous reach.

"In time all souls are progressively perfected. They become

able to recognize truths inaccessible to them on a lower level of consciousness.

"A person whose life has been directed toward advancing the welfare of his fellow men, rather than solely toward egoistic goals, on the other side will have a better point of departure on the road to fulfillment. He will have a head start, so to speak, on a person who has confined himself to cheating, betraying, or perhaps destroying others.

"The supernatural world, exactly like the one on earth, is the way we make it. There no negative influences are found, of course. Encouragement, inspiration, and wisdom can be absolutely counted on. In other words, there's nothing there to lose, everything to gain."

Daily Helen Aintree receives visitors, who come to her for a variety of reasons. Most of them are bent on knowing whether such and such a person, someone who ought not to have been obliterated by death, does in fact still exist and how he is faring. Others want messages transmitted near and far. And besides these there are many others—from simple folk to prominent scientists—who want to be thoroughly informed on the method used by this interesting woman in making her journey into the world after death. She gives a description of this method, which in summary goes as follows:

"At first I go to a very quiet room. Only a soft half-light comes through the drawn curtains. I sit down in a comfortable chair with my back stretched out, so as to relax completely. I then have to put myself in a sort of trance in order to loosen and undo the bonds the mundane and the supernatural body. With a certain breathing rhythm—by drawing in deep breaths and letting them out through my mouth—I gather all my spiritual strength together and concentrate with all my might on the one goal: my journey into the beyond. It's only a short while before I feel, without any sense of fear, my astral body detaching itself from me and setting out on the journey.

"I see my body below me getting smaller and smaller, as if I were being lifted up a shaft filled with bright light. Experience has taught me that the best thing is to keep my gaze fixed upward, since otherwise I see frightful things unfolding on every side. The higher I rise, the more the figures and images lose their brutality, until finally all is peaceful. In this sphere I have reached my destination."

After this account the experiences of the American, the late Edgar Cayce, considered to be the most gifted clairvoyant and miracle healer of the age, should not go unmentioned:

"I see myself as a tiny point detached from my earthly body, and I perceive this body as lying motionless before me. Somehow I become aware that I am trapped in an oppressive darkness, and I have a feeling of being terribly alone. But suddenly I become aware of a beam of white light. As the small point that I now am, I struggle upward toward the source of the light and know that I must reach it or be lost.

"While I am ascending the path of light, I become ever more conscious that I am passing through different levels on which there is a great deal of commotion. On the lowest level I see vague but frightful shapes, grotesque forms like those seen in nightmares. Then, on all sides, monsters begin to appear, parts of whose bodies was incongruously large."

Cayce goes on to describe more changes of scene and mood until he finally reaches his goal. Once there, he can relate to others. They are the ones with whom he feels a spiritual affinity.

But to return to Helen Aintree, she describes one of her recent excursions into the beyond this way:

"Mrs. Beale, who had been widowed a short time before, wanted to find out from me where her husband was and whether he was happy. Quite incidentally she mentioned that after his death she had searched in vain for a life insurance policy he had taken out years earlier.

"I felt sorry for this sad, old woman, and promised to help her. On the other hand, I made it clear that she was asking for something I simply could not guarantee. As I understand it, a particular person can be located in the beyond only after the highest plane of the supernatural journey has been attained. Often I found myself on another plane or in another sphere, and it could take years and years to make a contact with her dead husband.

"People who lived a peaceful life and had a set of values, who were not solely devoted to money and success, can be found on a plane that one might call the haven of peace, a place where other souls will give counsel in preparing for further ascent.

"In all events, it is very hard for these beings to remember the details of their mortal existence. This also holds for mundane things, which seem very important to survivors. Winning at bingo or finding an insurance policy doesn't count very much with these souls. Happy times, such as their wedding trip or a reunion with dear friends, seem to live on in their memory, and likewise moments of despair—as if such experiences had been a living part of themselves.

"However, in the case of Mrs. Beale, who wanted information on the whereabouts of the document I have just mentioned, I was lucky. Sidney Beale had already been trying to get in touch with his wife, to tell her where the policy was. The importance of it must have lingered in his memory.

"I found Mr. Beale very quickly, for the reason that his desire to make contact with his wife was as strong as my intention to find him. He told me that the document was in the bottom of an old cupboard in the garden shed and that I might pass on this information.

"The next day Mrs. Beale in Brighton was in receipt of this message from me."

It worked. Mrs. Beale actually found the policy in the place named by Helen Aintree.

"It's simply unbelievable," was the fifty-four-year-old widow's comment on this remarkable incident. "No one knew where the policy was, and Mrs. Aintree couldn't have found it by telepathy. Sidney was the only one who knew where it was hidden."

But Mrs. Aintree herself is never surprised when she gets messages of this nature. She is also convinced that she is not the only one who has the ability to travel to the realm of the dead.

In his book *The Life Beyond Death* (New York: Berkley, 1972), Arthur Ford describes his experience of the beyond:

> . . . I was floating in the air above my bed. I could see my body but had no interest in it. There was a feeling of peace, a sense that all was well. Now I lapsed into a timeless blank. When I recovered consciousness, I found my self floating through space, without effort, without any sense that I possessed a body as I had known my body. Yet I was I *myself*.
>
> Now there appeared a green valley with mountains on all sides, illuminated everywhere by a brilliance of light and color impossible to describe. People were coming toward me from all around, people I had known and thought of as "dead." I knew them all. Many I had not thought of for years, but it seemed that everyone I had ever cared about was there to greet me. Recognition was more by personality than by physical attributes. They had changed ages. Some who had passed on in old age were now young, and some who had passed on while children had now matured.
>
> I have often had the experience of traveling to a foreign country, being met by friends and introduced to the local customs and taken to places of interest any visitor to the country would want to see. It was like that now. Never have I been so royally greeted. I was shown all the things they seemed to think I should see. My memory of these places is as clear as my impression of the countries I have visited in this life: The beauty of a sunrise viewed from a peak in the Swiss Alps, the Blue Grotto of Capri, the hot, dusty roads of India are no more powerfully etched in my memory than the spirit world in which I knew myself to be. Time has never dimmed the memory of it. It is as vivid and real as anything I have ever known.
>
> There was one surprise: Some people I would have expected to see here were not present. I asked about them. In the instant of asking a thin transparent film seemed to fall over my eyes. The light grew dimmer, and colors lost

their brilliance. I could no longer see those to whom I had been speaking, but through a haze I saw those for whom I had asked. They, too, were real, but as I looked at them, I felt my own body become heavy; earthly thoughts crowded into my mind. It was evident to me that I was being shown a lower sphere. I called to them; they seemed to hear me, but I could not hear a reply. Then it was over. A gentle being who looked like a symbol of eternal youth, but radiated power and wisdom, stood by me. "Don't worry about them," he said. "They can come here whenever they want to if they desire it more than anything else."

Everyone here was busy. They were continually occupied with mysterious errands and seemed to be very happy. Several of those to whom I had been bound by close ties in the past did not seem to be much interested in me. Others I had known only slightly became my companions. I understood that this was right and natural. The law of affinity determined our relationships here.

At some point—I had no awareness of time—I found myself standing before a dazzling white building. Entering, I was told to wait in an enormous anteroom. They said I was to remain here until some sort of disposition had been made of my case. Through wide doors I could glimpse two long tables with people sitting at them and talking—about me. Guiltily I began an inventory of my life. It did not make a pretty picture. The people at the long tables were also reviewing the record, but the things that worried me did not seem to have much interest for them. The conventional sins I was warned about as a child were hardly mentioned. But there was sober concern over such matters as selfishness, egotism, stupidity. The word "dissipation" occurred over and over—not in the usual sense of intemperance but as waste of energies, gifts, and opportunities. On the other side of the scale were some simple, kindly things such as we all do from time to time without thinking them of much consequence. The "judges" were trying to make out the main *trend* of my life. They mentioned my having failed to accomplish "what he *knew* he had to finish." There was a purpose for me, it seemed, and I had not fulfilled it. There was a plan for my life, and I had misread the blueprint. "They're going to send me back," I thought, and I didn't like it. Never did I discover who these people were. They repeatedly used the word "record"; perhaps the Akashic Record of the ancient mystery schools—the great universal spiritual sound track on which all events are recorded.

When I was told I had to return to my body . . . I was standing before a door. I knew if I passed through it, I would be back where I had been. I decided I wouldn't go. Like a spoiled child in a tantrum, I pushed my feet against the wall and fought. There was a sudden sense of hurtling through space. I opened my eyes and looked into the face of a nurse. I had been in a coma for more than two weeks.

People who reach beyond their own self, their own innermost being, into the beyond are common in India. For a number of years, the forty-year-old Swami Rama carried out experiments that attracted great notice both in his homeland and abroad. This yogi, who came from Badrinath, near the Tibetan border, had learned the secrets of being buried alive at a yoga school. In making these experiments, which were supposed to open the door to the beyond to his soul, he induced in himself a state of suspended animation. This artificial tetany was intended to reduce his body's energy needs, to a point where he could live for long periods without food or water. Nothing but a limited supply of air was provided in the simulated grave. The experiments lasted twenty-one days all together. The yogi Swami Rama terminated the experiments himself and retained a precise memory of the faces he had seen.

"In the beyond I had the task of investigating the possibilities of a world peace," the yogi explained. "I learned that the chances for such a peace are good. Although very critical and dangerous days, weeks, and months still lie ahead, things will not come to a third world war.

"We cannot count on the great men of our time to change from one day to the next. A tiger does not become a lamb overnight. Everything takes time. But with enough patience and strength of conviction even the heart of an evil spirit, as well as a tiger, can be changed."

Swami Rama did not say how he became privy to such intelligence in the beyond. But his are comforting words. And they come from a man who for nine days, of his own will, was buried under the ground without food and water, this while looking deep into himself so as to be able to assert: "I am above time and space!"

CHORUS OF THE DEAD

We dead, we dead are a greater commotion
Than you down on earth, than you on the ocean!
We plowed the fields with patience and pain,
You swung the sickle and you garnered the grain,
And what we completed, what put to leaven
Still fills rushing fountains high up in heaven,
And all our loving and hating and bane
Still pulses on in your mortal vein.
And what for us was lawful relation
To it is still subject all earthly mutation,
And our music, creations, all lyric flight
Competes for the laurel in a radiant light.
Your goals remain ours in immortal region—
Therefore honor and sacrifice; For our number is legion.

CONRAD FERDINAND MEYER (1825–1898)

16

The Living Dead

SHORTLY BEFORE WORLD WAR II, word came from various countries about frightful experiments in which decapitated animals and detached heads were kept alive. But the hints and scraps of information leaking out of laboratory seclusion were not enough to make the world sit up and pay attention.

Meanwhile, the skilled hands of daring surgeons and the sophisticated knowledge of clever technicians were producing devices that permitted headless bodies and bodiless heads to live and function.

Oxygen-saturated blood was pumped into the brain of detached heads by artificial hearts. Animals deprived of hearts smelled and tasted, moved their eyes and breathed. Heads detached from the torso reacted. In other animals, in experiments using a system of tubes implanted in the trunk, the heart, which normally is controlled automatically by the brain, was regulated in its beat by a motor.

Who can say whether the first experiment of this sort known in Europe would have turned out, as it did, to be a resounding failure if its author, the French surgeon Jean Laborde, had had the benefit of modern knowledge and technique?

At the time—nearly one hundred years ago—this Paris surgeon united the head of an executed murderer with the circulatory system of a dog. A trace of life was observed in the severed head, but this alone was not enough to guarantee the success Laborde had expected for his bold undertaking. In any case, his experiment paved the way for many horror stories and films, and at the same time, to some extent, spurred other more or less ingenious experimenters to build laboratories in out-of-the-way cellar vaults for similar ghastly ventures. Yet in later years the creation of creatures with automatic brains who could be activated by electrical impulses transmitted from a hundred yards away continued to be classified as so much science fiction.

Today, almost a century after the Frenchman Laborde's unsuccessful experiment, stories of this kind suddenly acquired a practical foundation when an American professor, Robert White, presented the world public with a medical sensation that put even the work of the famous heart-transplant surgeon, Dr. Christiaan Barnard of Capetown, South Africa, in the shade. With his thrilling head transplant, Dr. White ushered in a new era in the field of brain surgery. He began by successfully grafting the head of a rhesus monkey onto another monkey body.

This neurosurgeon, who works with an astounding team at the brain research center at the university in Cleveland, defends his experiments, which already include about one hundred transplants, on the grounds that they are "necessary training for operating on humans."

In White's view these transplanted animal heads function like any other, and he is convinced that his ultimate goal is now within reach: to sew onto a human being with a sound body but hopelessly damaged brain the head of a body ruined beyond salvation but kept artificially alive.

Professor White began his investigations years ago by carefully removing the brain of an anesthetized monkey. He then attached this brain mass to a heart-lung machine, while making sure, by special devices, that its blood supply showed no anomalies. Later he dissected another monkey head in such fashion that one eye remained attached to the brain. He found that the pupil of this eye expanded and contracted in response to light.

In these experiments one important factor had to be clarified—the input and output of blood to the brain. It is accomplished in nature by four large arteries and four large veins. Was it possible to take two of these blood vessels out of circulation for a time without destroying the brain's blood supply? A long series of experiments yielded hoped-for results: two arteries and two veins were sufficient. With that established, precious time could be saved for the operation.

Professor White, with the assistance of five other doctors, has done actual head transplants on two-year-old rhesus monkeys. The operation takes about eight hours. The skin on the neck of the anesthetized animal is cut away in broad strips, after which all the supporting tissue is excised, leaving only the cervical vertebrae, the esophagus, the trachea, and the main blood vessels. The trachea is attached to an artificial breathing machine so that the lungs have an assured oxygen supply. After carefully breaking open the cervical vertebrae, the spinal cord is disconnected by a cut through this thick bundle of nerve tracts, thus interrupting the transmission of commands from head to body. All but the essential blood vessels are ligated so that no blood loss occurs.

After two cervical vertebrae are broken apart, the four main blood vessels between head and body are successively provided with plastic inserts.

Meanwhile, a second monkey has been anesthetized so that its head can be similarly removed. The detached head is then attached to the torso of this second animal, a procedure entailing no great difficulties, because of the plastic tubes previously inserted.

Less than two hours after the operation has begun, the head on the strange body emerges from anesthesia. The now composite monkey opens its eyes, is able to see and hear, move its lips, and chew. Its capacity for reaction has not been diminished. It can move its face parts, but not turn its head. Because the head is tied in with the new body only by blood vessels, with the nerves serving communication severed, the torso and limbs remain paralyzed. These experiments are continuing. At present the animals used in them have been brought to a stage comparable to that of a person who has had his neck broken in an accident and is doomed to spend the rest of his life in bed with body and limbs paralyzed.

It is just such tragic cases that give brain surgeon White

the incentive to go on with his work. Naturally, he is well aware of the ethical problems involved.

The reaction of medical science—leaving aside massive hostility from the antivivisectionists—has been far from positive. The same holds for the philosophers and theologians. Many of these people regard this whole complex of effort as a brutish assault on nature, as defiance of divine providence, although White himself is known to be a practicing Roman Catholic.

Six months before publishing his results, in the fall of 1971, White made a trip to Rome. The Pope evinced a great interest in the details of the undertaking and the audience proceeded in an atmosphere of understanding, if not of encouragement. This at least suggested that if in time there were human head transplants, there would be no objection or protest on the part of the Vatican.

Many shudder and recoil when we dwell on such accounts. And yet even more terrible things have happened. There are monsters who have treated human life as if it were a stick of wood. One has no desire to go into the details of where and how and why. But the results must be reported; what human heads have felt and described—human heads bereft of a trunk, robbed from the body in executing a court finding of insanity, heads mounted on a mechanism of tubes, heads whose circulatory systems were maintained by means of a tubular system in which ingeniously refined solutions were circulated.

"I knew it was all up with me. I had told myself it would be over quickly, and afterward . . .

"I heard everything you were saying—how you insulted me to the end. I saw everything when you removed my head. I felt everything as long as there was still a drop of my own blood left in me. And suddenly I was thinking again—because other blood was flowing in me.

"I was horribly afraid when I went under the knife—when I felt the dull heavy blow on my neck and thought it was all over. I wasn't afraid of death itself, but of dying, of the knife.

"But all I was thinking was, it's the finish for me . . .

"Now I'm here again, existing and yet not existing. But I know I've had it . . .

"Terrible . . . terrible . . .

"I'm hurting . . .

"Get it over with. Just let me die . . .

"I haven't a body any more, no arms or legs. But I can hear what you're saying and I hear you laughing and I'm suffering . . ."

The foregoing is an excerpt from a report on such an experiment.

In earlier times executioners have explained in long expositions that when a man is decapitated all feelings vanish from head and body by the instant emptying of blood from the head and brain centers. If a head shows movement after being severed from the torso, this is not proof of the continuance of psychic life in the head.

Doctors agree with such expert opinion. The fall of the heavy ax coupled the psychic agitation immediately before the impact totally cuts off all reflex activity. The assault on the nervous system is so enormous that normal functioning is out of the question.

The mental tension that completely possesses the brain on the one hand distracts the attention from physical feelings and on the other paralyzes the capacity to feel—all these things tend to make execution painless.

Such are the carefully considered reflections of people wanting to free themselves from blood-guilt for deeds done in the official line of duty, or ease the conscience of those who pronounced the death sentence and thereafter repeatedly sought moral support from others for what they had done.

But experiments in which animal heads were kept alive without benefit of bodies—heads able to smack their lips and know thirst, able to hear the voice of their master and to show fear—these experiments as well as the gruesome ones with human heads (which were also done in China thousands of years ago) contradict everything that executioners and defenders of capital punishment maintain about pain.

Some time ago, at a professional convention in southern

Europe, a physiologist seriously advanced the proposition that
sooner or later robot brains would be created—robots of flesh
and blood, brains that could not die.

"People wear out. The organs become fatigued and can no
longer perform as they once could. People with outstanding
qualities, with excellent mental capacities, die from some triv-
ial physical injury, with completely sound lungs and with a
healthy brain. Today there are people who leave their eyes to
an eye bank. Others will their brain to the universities. Why,
then, should people with superior brains leave them dead to
humanity? Why not leave the whole head while the brain is
still alive and functioning? They could continue to live intact
until the body gave out. But at the moment of natural death,
the robot service would come into play. It would assume control of the deceased's brain a few seconds after he had
expired, introducing into it an artificial circulation making possible cerebral function without human blood and without a
body."

These are shattering considerations. But questing man, not
being able to find what he is looking for in his artificial elec-
tronic brains, ventures further and further into the fantastic.
Of course, what this physiologist proposed is not feasible with
current technology.

If, before they died, highly intelligent people placed at the
disposal of psychological research residually functioning brains
that could be stimulated to keep on performing, this would
put on a rational basis all we have been trying to clarify by a
laborious collection of material from all over the world.

Brains would be then on hand that were not allowed to die,
and these might make it possible for those who delve in these
difficult fields to follow every last shadow of thought and feeling of a person or a soul from this world on its passage into
the beyond.

We have seen that headless trunks can function and that
having the head attached to a body is not necessary for some
mental activity to continue. It is also true that the diaphragm
and solar plexus develop auxiliary "brains" that, under certain

circumstances, are able to maintain lifelike function under the direction of a motor.

Artificial hearts, artificially supported heads—these point the way to the robot brains we have just, with a shudder, heard about. They represent the possibility of creating brains that cannot die.

The purpose here has been to tell about people who came back from the dead and informed about the other side. But the physical side could not be avoided, since doing so would have excluded the resurrection of the dead, the existence of beings with artificial hearts.

Now, what can be taken for real in these accounts of a genuine or alleged beyond? One thing in this compilation that more than once caught the eye was this: Every subject felt that he had experienced something unique. This was especially true in those cases where, at the time, there was other evidence, besides the subject's reporting of it, for the existence of a state between life and death. On the other hand, in our view uniform manifestations may be explained by popular fads. They may likewise appear when nationally or regionally colored traditions are firmly anchored in the unconscious, thus permitting images reflecting this uniformity to arise during a deep psychological experience.

It may, therefore, be said that a strictly personal experience as described verbatim by a person brought to life from death has the highest claim to credibility, with the obvious qualification that an individual experience can never be made subject to control or testing.

All other experiences, like visions of a religious character, are colored according to tradition.

Shall we conclude from this that the boundary between this world and the next can be crossed and re-crossed, if only in exceptional cases? Undoubtedly there are and there will continue to be people who are firmly convinced that they can recall a sojourn in another world. But this recall is and will remain subjective.

There are devices in use that can record human brain

waves. These brain waves, the variations of which are being measured ever more finely and carefully, one day will provide a key to the identification of concepts and words. We will then have moved a good way toward the objective investigation of psychic events.

In other words, we have to make thoughts visible, represent them so graphically that their translation into a visual image will precisely reflect what is going on in the subject's brain cells, and with that have an idea of what is occurring in consciousness.

But naturally these experiments at best are only preliminary to the study of psychological experiences at the threshold, or in the beyond itself.

With these experiments, then, we approach ever closer to the truth—assuming there is an objective truth in this context. For the dogma that compresses life after death within a completely definite frame, cleverly invented doctrines that are supposed to show a sure path for getting safely into the beyond—these offer no proof that they are right or that the context from which they evolved can stand up to the critique that research someday will bring to bear.

If, in our psychic experiences, our spiritual travail, and our quest for the truth, we are dealing only with cell function in the cerebral cortex, then, viewed logically, with the means available today we can approach only to the threshold of the beyond, or at the most venture no more than tentative probes into the other side.

But if there is something more than simple cell function, something that cannot be forced into aforementioned theoretical contexts about this world and the other world, then it becomes the task of psychic research, of parapsychology, always proceeding from cell function in the brain, to cross the threshold, to tear down the barrier and to provide certain knowledge of what lies on the other side to all concerned.

So long as neither physiological research, with its refined wave measurements, and parapsychology, with its ingenious outwitting of psychosomatic function to attain small certainties about the beyond, has yet reached its final goal, we shall rest content (in a spirit of modesty proper to those who recognize the limitations of their means) with verbatim reports brought to our notice from time to time from persons who themselves have stood on the threshold between here and out there.

Still, so long as we do not know what is on the other side, we must believe, each in his own way and according to his psychological needs. We must believe until perhaps someday a later generation opens up avenues that will make certainty out of our belief.

For we all long for this certainty. We long for it all the more in that with each passing hour, with each breath, we draw nearer to the brink from which we can never hope to find our way back. We cannot entertain the hope of being one of the few to whom fate, actually or allegedly, accords a view of both sides. We simply stand here and strain to hear what might be going on in the beyond, a region from which only rarely does a voice penetrate across to us. And even then this voice can be interpreted only by those whom nature has endowed with an inner ear that can hearken and understand what others, who do not know how to hear, are aware of as only a faint whispering.

17

The Final Balance

IT WOULD SEEM NECESSARY by way of conclusion to touch on some basic observations in respect of physiological man after death. In a few pertinent words the Dutch physiologist Professor R. Engelmann states the events of life and death as viewed from the standpoint of the countless cells of which we are made:

"The cells live together, but they die separately. Somatic life, the collective life of a complete organism in its particularities, can exist then only if all cell groups, tissues, and organs are alive and totally active. Their harmonious accord, the maintenance of their relationships, the strict observance of their reciprocal states—these are the prerequisites of their collective life. The body, therefore, is to be compared to a watch, the movement of which breaks down if there is serious damage at any point in it. The whole then comes to a stop. Death must come sooner or later, that is, somatic death, the death of the organism, if not of each single cell group."

It is understandable that each group and organization of cells must suffer as soon as the organic balance is disturbed. Nonetheless, groups die by degrees, one after the other. Some groups have greater resistance, and they perish separately.

Death takes hold first in the brain cells, these suffering more than the others from circulatory stoppage. Into play here come the experiments of Dr. Konstantin Hossmann of which we have already given a thorough account. If the blood circulation is not successfully restored, the brain will become susceptible to the death march of the cells, a march that, as we know today, can last for hours. As for the muscles, they can react for many hours to artificial stimulation.

Many years ago Professor Dr. Henry de Varigny of Paris talked about the theme of death and dying. He made the following comments:

"For the scientific observer, who confronts the dead organism in a far from romantic state of mind, death gradually destroys a body built up slowly in the course of years, and it destroys a personality that has taken years to become a human being. As far as we can scientifically judge, it puts a quietus to events whose beginning, to be sure, we see, but which did not always exist.

"Since we have no positive, secure data on the possibility of existence after death, and since we do not know whether the spirit—which seems to be so closely bound up with our material organization and which organization is partially conditioned by it, so that no one can deny its influence—is destroyed along with the body, then everyone is free to embrace the belief that pleases him and on which he can make up his mind.

"He is even permitted to believe that the spirit—which developed with the body, with it became stronger and weaker, and for which we have no evidence of previous existence—can survive the body and lead an independent, eternal existence.

"But all this will always be only a belief, a hope, which cannot hold its own against logic and reasoning.

"Here science recognizes its inadequacy and cloaks itself in a discreet silence; for if it were to speak, it would be stepping out of its role. However, if assailed with questions which move science notwithstanding to give answers, questions eliciting the scientific attitude toward the plausibility of opinions based on belief, what the scientist would say then would be anything but encouraging.

"In any event, it is wiser not to ask science at all; its duty is to destroy illusions, not to support them. Herein lies its power. Also its weakness."

But we shall close with a word from Arthur Koestler:

"That there is only matter and no spirit is a highly illogical proposition, far from the findings of modern physics, which show that there is no matter in the traditional sense of the concept." This is yet another aspect of the problem to which we can point, an aspect indicating how mobile, how uncertain, is the borderline between being and not-being.

Bibliography

Das Ägyptische Totenbuch, Otto Wilhelm Barth Verlag GmbH, Weilheim/Obb.

Ist keiner aus dem Jenseits zurückgekommen? G. Pasquali, Verlag Siegfried Hacker, Gröbenzell b. Munich.

Königin Friederike, Erfahrungen, Rainer Wunderlich Verlag Hermann Leins, Tübingen and Stuttgart

Life Without Death? Nils O. Jacobson, M.D., Delacorte Press/Seymour Lawrence, New York

The Life Beyond Death, Arthur Ford, Berkley, New York

Das Tibetanische Totenbuch, Walter-Verlag, Olten and Freiburg.

Grenzgebiete der Wissenschaft, A 6010 Innsbruck, Maximilianstr. 6.

Ferdinand Zahlner, *Kleines Lexikon der Paranormalogie.* Herausgegeben von Prof. Dr. Andreas Resch, Verlag Josef Kral/Arensberg

Der Traum im Heilsplan Gottes. Andreas Resch, Herder Verlag, Freiburg (out of print)

Im Kraftfeld des christlichen Weltbildes, Andreas Resch, Schöningh Verlag, Paderborn

Probleme der Parapsychologie, Andreas Resch/G. Frei, Schöningh Verlag, Paderborn

Welt, Mensch und Wissenschaft morgen, Andreas Resch, Schöningh Verlag, Paderborn

Der kosmische Mensch, Andreas Resch, Schöningh Verlag, Paderborn (in Vorbereitung)